Please return to
Barbara J. Landis 362-2686
415 Rose St.

Big & Beautiful
Overcoming Fatphobia

Ruthanne Olds

Photographs by Jon Olds
Designed by Robert Hickey

ACROPOLIS BOOKS LTD.
Washington, D.C.

Dedicated

To Jon, my best friend, partner, and husband—Thanks for helping me through the tears and the triumph.

To Barbara Deane, my teacher and mentor—Without you this book would still be in my head.

To Sandi Gostin and my other friends—Thanks for the support.

To Mom and our fat family tree—Without you this book would not have been necessary.

To Kathleen Hughes and the gang at Acropolis Books—Thanks for believing in my idea.

To the late Edith Head and to Carole Shaw—and all the other great people who have touched my life.

Thank you

© Copyright 1982 by Acropolis Books Ltd.
All rights reserved. Except for the inclusion of brief quotations in a review, no part of this book may be reproduced or utilized in any form or by any means, electronic or mechanical, including photocopying, recording or by an information storage and retrieval system, without permission in writing from the publisher.

ACROPOLIS BOOKS LTD
Colortone Building, 2400 17th St., N.W.,
Washington, D.C. 20009

Library of Congress Cataloging in Publication Data

Olds, Ruthanne, 1952-
  Big & Beautiful.

  Includes index.
  1. Beauty, Personal. 2. Clothing and dress. 3. Nutrition. 4. Obesity—Social aspects. I. Title.
RA778.035   646´.34´088081   82-6724
  ISBN 0-87491-088-9   AACR2

Printed in the United States of American by
COLORTONE PRESS *Creative Graphics Inc.*
Washington, D.C., 20009

ATTENTION: Schools and Corporations
  ACROPOLIS books are available at quantity discounts with bulk purchase for educational, business, or sales promotional use. For information, please write to: SPECIAL SALES DEPARTMENT, ACROPOLIS BOOKS LTD., 2400 17th ST., NW, WASHINGTON, D.C. 20009

Are There Acropolis Books
You Want But Cannot Find In Your Local Stores?
  You can get any Acropolis book title in print. Simply send title and retail price, plus $.50 per copy to cover mailing and handling costs for each book desired. District of Columbia residents add applicable sales tax. Enclose check or money order only, no cash please, to: ACROPOLIS BOOKS LTD., 2400 17th ST., NW, WASHINGTON, D.C. 20009. OR SEND FOR OUR COMPLETE CATALOGUE OF ACROPOLIS BOOKS.

Preface

Before you reach for another diet book, read this book. You owe it to yourself to check out an alternative to the same old yo-yo syndrome.

If you think thin is the answer, you are never going to be able to stay that way unless you learn how to like yourself—**all** your selves. That includes your fat self as well as your thin self.

If you're serious about improving your life, at least learn what the problem really is.

CONTENTS

1   The Discovery of Fatphobia 9

2   Freedom from Fatphobia 31

3   Where Do You Start: Attitude .. 43

4   The Language of Image 53

5   The Language of Design . 75

Big & Beautiful

6 Balance and Emphasis: The New Rules 91

7 Developing a Personal Style . . . 105

8 The Language of Fashion 125

9 Becoming a Smart Image Shopper 137

10 Sounds Good So Far, But Does It Work? 153

11 Instead of an Eating Program, Try a People Program . . . 167

12 Fatphobia Awareness Training: Finally Something That Works . 179

Appendix A
Exactly What Can A FAT Group Do for You? 201
   The First Meeting
   A Typical Meeting
   Becoming a Leader
   Developing Topics

Appendix B
Other Topics 221

Appendix C
Directory of Stores 224

Index 232

Chapter 1

THE DISCOVERY OF FATPHOBIA

Fatphobia (fat-fo'be-a), n., the unrealistic fear, dread, hatred of being, becoming, or being associated with fat. Cause: social obsession with super youth, beauty, and thinness. Consequence: compulsive eating, anorexia nervosa, bulimia, preoccupation with unnecessary dieting by two-thirds of the population, billion dollar quack diet industry, and many lives wasted waiting for impossible physical perfection. Cure: self-respect through raising of consciousness. Result: positive self-image.

WHY A BOOK ABOUT FATPHOBIA?

Why would an attractive, educated woman who has achieved a respectable degree of success spend two years researching a book about fat, especially during one of the most diet and exercise conscious times in history?

Why? Because I was sick of everyone I knew complaining about being on a diet or being fat. I resented being pressured into believing I had to be part of the diet madness to be normal. Dieting is a regular recreational pastime—I wouldn't be surprised if it became an olympic event.

I felt forced to play a "Beat the Clock and Scale" game. The media proclaimed a fifteen year old the ideal Woman of the Eighties. God help us—she's not even going to be a woman until the eighties are over. If we're going to declare flat-chested, hipless figures as the standard of female perfection, then let's admire women like Katharine Hepburn, Gloria Steinem, or Nancy Reagan. At least they've done more than star in softcore kiddie porn.

Sure, I'm mad. I'm fed up with the farce. I resent being told I'm ugly, boring, and over the hill. I'm not even thirty. I'm tired of being told I have to reduce to be considered human. I don't have to be thin to be happy, healthy, or attractive.

How many times have you been told by someone that they're dieting to get healthier? Then you ask them what kind of nutritional program they're on and they say something like hard boiled eggs and grapefruit juice. Give me a break. Americans aren't dieting for their health, they're dieting because they think losing weight will make them look younger and sexier.

Formal balance

A formally balanced look with the symmetrical jewel collar, detailed dress, and hair pulled back evenly on both sides.

Informal balance

The look is balanced but informal with the loosely tied scarf pulled to one side and the hair pulled back only on one side.

Turn to page 82 for more information on how to use balance to enhance your image.

Big & Beautiful

11

Everyone wants to fit in. We all want to be part of what's going on. That's great if it keeps people thinking young, but we've got a problem when we make youthfulness a stereotype.

I'm not alone. There is a growing rumble of discontent being heard. People are tired of Madison Avenue making mountains of money by playing on our vanity, selling us youth, sex, and the impossible dream in a bottle. The media screams young and sexy. Most people respond, "That's fine for the kids, but what about me?"

Do you really believe the only people who are truly happy and successful are the skinnies? I don't. I've earned my wrinkles and padding. So have you. They represent a lot of rewarding life experience. I expect to be appreciated and respected for my personal worth, not for my dress size. I'm rebelling against fatphobia. So are a lot of other people. I'm fighting back. So can you. Stop being the victim of a media campaign and start living a fun, productive life.

Big & Beautiful began when I discovered fatphobia. I became furious at the thought of another diet. I was tired of seeing diet experts fleecing the public. I couldn't face another book aimed at fat people written by a skinny author who refers to "overweight people" as though we're another species. Aren't there any books that support a *choice* about body size?

I searched for months and came up with about a dozen titles . . . a dozen compared to the *hundreds* on dieting. Talk about a stacked deck! We deserve the chance to see another side of the body size question, but few people have been given an opportunity to talk about anything except dieting. So I asked myself, what's the one thing you're really an expert on, besides dieting? Being fat. I never dreamed it could be an asset. I always thought of it as being like some kind of ancient curse on my family. Here was my chance to share the truth: fat people have the right to live. We are as normal as everyone else.

That is to say we would be as normal as everyone else if society would stop believing in the cliches concerning fatness. Wherever I talked with women (and a few men) about body size, I heard the same message. One of the first people I interviewed summed up our plight perfectly.

"I am so glad to have somebody say something, do something to make people realize we aren't freaks or oddities. I'm a person who just wants to be accepted. I'm like Joe Blow next door. I may be larger, but I have the same feelings. Most of us are unhappy enough without having the rest of the world looking down their noses at us."

This peppy grandmother with sparkling blue eyes said it all. People might argue that a good-natured joke won't do us any harm. Perhaps the name-calling and joking doesn't hurt some, but for the hundreds of fat people with whom I've spoken, being fat hasn't been fun, much less funny.

LIFE FOR FAT AMERICANS

What has life been like for fat Americans these last few decades? While the picture I paint in this first chapter may be depressing at times, don't despair. *Big & Beautiful* will show you how to overcome the problems common to all fat people. The attitudes causing these problems can be changed. They are changing now. But before you can change, you must be able to recognize how fatphobia is affecting your life.

I want to thank the people with the courage to share their stories. They have consented to do so in the hope that this shared knowledge will help rid us of fatphobia's cruelly demeaning and destructive power. I guaranteed anonymity so that everyone could speak freely and without embarrassment. A friend painstakingly transcribed each quote from their taped comments. Sometimes the tapes were inaudible due to the laughter and excitement of being able to finally talk about our darkest secret.

You'll be amazed at how much their stories are *your* story. Pay attention to the number of experiences we share. We are not freaks. We are just people trying to cope. This is what fatphobia has done to me . . . and probably you, too.

Ruthanne's Story

I was a normal kid—skinny, sickly, and learning disabled. Then, when I was in third grade, I had my tonsils taken out. Almost overnight, I became a healthy, robust, active . . . and *fat* child. Everyone in my family is big—my mom, dad, brother, and grandmothers. Considering our Dutch, Irish, German, and Lithuanian heritage, it was natural for me to be large, too, but this didn't matter to my cruel classmates.

What's it like to be a fat little kid? It's hell. You're ridiculed and excluded. I can remember thinking I'd rather be dead than fat. A couple of events in the fourth grade seemed to make it worse. My mother gave me a permanent that frizzled and I had to start wearing glasses. My hair was a mess. It had been cut so short I looked like a boy. Here I was, a big, fat kid with frizzy, flaming red hair, hundreds of freckles, and thick glasses with ridiculous French poodles on the frame's. I was known as the fat four-eyed freak. I wasn't invited to slumber parties or Girl Scouts, and I was the last person picked for a team.

There are always a few of us in every school. Kids call us "its" or "things." To survive you either get tough or you retreat. I developed a tough exterior and a vulnerable interior. After a few years of abuse, you learn to internalize the rejection as being your fault. You know you are not different, but, you believe the stupid labels that mark you as a failure.

Was my story an isolated one? Did I lead an abnormal, deprived childhood? Hardly. Linda, a tall and big woman, recalls similar childhood experiences.

Linda's Story

"Kids are cruel to begin with. It starts in grade school. My whole self-image went right down the tube when I was eleven years old. We were playing slip-and-slide, and my nickname was 'Fatty, Fatty, Two-by-four.' As you get older, you keep hearing your parents and friends say 'Can't you lose weight?' or 'How come you're so fat?' I remember in seventh and eighth grades and I wasn't that heavy then, they stuck signs on my back that said 'Kick me, I'm fat.' A boy used to throw rocks at me because I was fat. That's the only reason he threw them."

Beth's Story

Beth, once a big woman, tells of her childhood misery. "I've been dieting since I was nine. They called me 'The Blob' enough times that I came in the house crying. When my mother wanted to know why, I asked her if I was fat. She told me I was just pleasingly plump. Then she called the principal and asked that the kids be stopped from harassing me. The principal sent me to the school nurse. She sent me to the clinic. I lost thirty pounds. Fat is a painful subject for me."

Adults communicate the idea that being fat is not okay. One member of a discussion group on weight was quick to identify the problem. "You see some fat lady walking down the street and the parent says, 'Look at that slob.' The kids hear it and automatically think there is something wrong with that person."

My father affectionately referred to me as his "mutate." It was his subtle way of telling me I wasn't normal. My mother had ambivalent feelings about her fat daughter. She had a weight problem all her life, so she tried to cushion my ego from complete destruction. She armed me with clever sayings like "at least you look like you get enough to eat." But when she got mad, her true feelings surfaced. "Nobody will ever want to marry a fat, ugly thing like you." It's an awful feeling to know even your parents are embarrassed because you're not "normal."

If it hadn't been for my sixth grade teacher, I might have grown up to be a very hostile person. He must have been a fat four-eyed freak when he was little, because he made an effort to recognize my talents. I hated him at the time. I thought he was weird to like me when no one else did, but now I'm grateful he had the insight and compassion to care.

The summer before my first year in junior high, I grew several inches. Thanks to this newfound power, I slimmed down. I discovered the magical power of dieting.

All I had to do was stop eating, and I would lose weight. The answer was so simple. I couldn't believe I hadn't made the connection before. For the first time in what seemed like forever, I went back to school with a normal body.

Sara's Story

I discovered dieting on my own, but many youngsters are forced into dieting at ridiculously young ages. Sara's story is a good example of how overzealous parents put "the fear of fat" into us.

"When I was a child, my mother had me on every diet that ever came out in *Ladies' Home Journal.* Safflower oil, protein, no protein, cottage cheese, eggs. I mean, anything that came out in the *Journal,* I was on it. My mother even went so far as to call my girlfriends and ask that they report back to her. She'd say, 'I'm doing it for her own good. If she puts anything in her mouth that is not legal, I want to know, so that I can really find out if Sara's really overeating, or whether it just doesn't work.' Once she had me on this egg diet and at the end of a week, I had actually gained two pounds.

How much self-confidence can people develop if they never are allowed to learn how to trust themselves?

We pick up fatphobia messages from parents and our peer groups, but the biggest contributor to negative feelings toward fat are male/female relationships. If the first diet isn't the result of taunts endured as a child, it's almost certain to be the result of cupid's bow. The overwhelming pressure to conform during puberty forces many adolescents and teenagers to start the diet failure cycle. Why? Because most teenagers fear exactly what happened to Connie in her high school days.

Connie's Story

"I would never have admitted that I wasn't liked in school. It was too degrading. But I know I wasn't, mainly by the boys. I never once dated a boy that I went to school with. Every boy I went out with was either out of school or from a different school. They wouldn't be caught dead going out with me, and I wasn't big then. People always commented, "Pretty face, pretty hair," but still, there was not one boy who would have risked taking me out in high school. I didn't go to my senior prom. I didn't go to my junior ball. I stayed home and cried both times, and that hurt. Nothing has hurt as much as missing those dances."

In the same interview, Connie's sister spoke up. "I had the same thing, on a smaller scale, because I wasn't big. I tried out for cheerleaders and didn't make it, and I know it was because of my weight. Then I got it down. But it's the same thing."

Being a big girl in high school can also cause the opposite problem when it comes to men. I was rounder and more developed than my girlfriends. I was always able to pass as being older than I was. Older boys and men noticed me more than they noticed my peers. Even though I was normal, I always compared myself to other girls, and I tried to diet down to their size. I started dating older boys when I was fourteen. When I was fifteen, I almost married a nineteen year old boy. He always compared me to the Twiggy-sized girls popular at the time. He nagged me constantly about my weight, and I almost became anorexic trying to please him. We finally broke up. On the rebound, I got engaged to another, older man. Everything seemed perfect. I relaxed and started eating normally. He dropped me and married someone else because I got too fat.

Karen's Story

Karen shares a similar experience. "I've never been married, but I almost got married twice. I dieted for four months for my first fiance. All I had was Sego. I lost forty-five pounds. I wasn't that big anyway. I was heavy,

Discovery

but solid. When I lost weight, I looked nice, but this man made me feel grotesque. He said he didn't want to marry anyone who would have to wear a tent. I had no confidence. I felt ugly. He had the problem, I didn't. In the year we were engaged, I convinced myself that I should just crawl into a hole and stay there. I had no personality. I didn't feel attractive. Then I met someone and I really fell in love with him.

When he asked me to dance, I was so shocked that I couldn't look at him. I thought he must be blind. He was gorgeous. He made me feel like a human being again. Now I'm comfortable. I wear between a size 18 and 20. I have a large bone structure. I don't feel out of shape. I've accepted that I will always be big."

In my own case, I remember thinking I had lost control of my life. I became fanatical about my weight, and started believing that everything good depended on my being thin. I was a victim of "lookism." People were defining me by my appearance, and I rebelled. I ran away to San Francisco, several times, became a flower child, and tried drugs. I dated a lot. My weight fluctuated a lot. When things were going well, I stayed thin. When things weren't going so well, I ate to compensate. As I think back, I realize I judged my whole life by the difference of ten or twenty pounds.

Strange as it may sound, I became an overachiever to compensate for my poor self-image. I was on the debate team, was captain of the gym team, and active in student government. I wasn't happy dating just one boy, I wanted all the boys to notice me. I took a part-time job at a local fabric store so I could afford a car and nice clothes. I dreamed of becoming a famous fashion expert, so I learned everything I could about selling fabrics. While still in high school, I coordinated fashion shows and demonstrations, ran the notions department, lectured at schools, did all the display work, and ran a bridal department.

THE FIRSTBORN/OVERACHIEVER SYNDROME

Sandra Hunnicutt, a registered nurse in San Jose, California, has found that most of the women who take her body size acceptance class suffer from what she calls the firstborn/overachiever syndrome. Sandra has been teaching classes for seven years.

"One thing I have found to be a consistent phenomenon is that up until this class, 80 to 90 percent of each class were firstborn girls. Everyone in this class is a firstborn child, unless you don't count only children, those from families when there is an age difference of five years or between children, or those who are children of a second family. It all fits. You have to meet the expectations of your parents. You have to be perfect. You carry that into your adult life. You have to take care of everyone all the time. You have to make sure that no one is unhappy, that food is on the table, that you do everything perfectly. You're the perfect wife, mother, and career person—the whole thing."

Patty's Story

Patty, one of Sandra's students, explains why she fits the overachiever pattern.

"I learned that since boys were not attracted to me, one way I could get the recognition was to excel in school. I was the editor of the newspaper, star of the drama club, and all that stuff. What it left with me was the concept that unless I was excelling, I was not acceptable. I was certainly not acceptable as far as my looks. So there is really a lot of compensation that goes with being fat. I think that is really where fat women grow up thinking they have absolutely no right to be assertive. They don't have any rights. They can't tell someone that their feelings are hurt, because they aren't supposed to have those feelings."

Right before graduation, I lost twenty pounds as a symbolic gesture of passage. I planned to be married that August, and after graduation I spent all my free time preparing for the wedding. I made my dress and trousseau; dresses for the bridesmaids, my grandmother's and a couple of friends; worked full-time; and painted my mother's house. When I put on my wedding gown for the ceremony, it hung—I must have lost another twenty-five pounds.

All this frantic activity was probably an attempt to repress the feeling that my jailbreak marriage was a mistake. I wasn't ready to settle down, and he wasn't ready to leave his family. As soon as we started having problems, I comforted myself with food. When our landlady casually mentioned we could stay awhile after the baby came, I was shocked and hurt. What baby? I fled to Weight Watchers in terror.

I thought I had finally found the answer. I dropped down to my "normal" weight. I started feeling better about myself. Unfortunately, the pressures of working full-time, keeping house, going to school, and having an unemployed husband were too much for our immature marriage. We never saw a second anniversary. I prayed that finishing my degree in Fashion Merchandising would give me a new start.

It seemed I was always trying to diet, but not very hard. I'd overeat because of pleasure or stress, though food wasn't a constant preoccupation. Until my first marriage, my weight problem was not that serious. The pressures of married life made me a hard-core compulsive eater. I tried to block out my feelings with an orgy of oral gratification. Unfortunately, food can never solve problems that are caused by other needs.

Sharon's Story

The onset of compulsive eating is often associated with a personal crisis. Sharon, an unhappily married legal assistant, tried to "eat away" her problems. "Before we were married, I weighed 128 pounds. By the time we married, I weighed 138. I started eating compulsively when I got my engagement ring. There were three fast-food places, and I'd go to all three. I don't know why I did it.

"I'd been married before; it lasted ten months. Then I experienced freedom. I was thin and happy. Everything in my life was going well.

"I think I held out for security, I was scared. We got married and he started complaining about my weight. At 138, I was not obese. But he was body conscious. He thought a thin wife was a symbol of his manhood. He wanted to be able to show me off. Over the next nine years, I became what he saw me to be—I got up to 210 pounds."

Susan's Story

Thirty-four-year-old Susan discovered that the struggle to lose a few pounds in order to catch a certain person's eye can easily become a lifelong struggle.

"I decided to go on my first diet for the benefit of a young man. I felt he rejected me after I lost the weight, so I became engaged on the rebound. I'm sure I got pregnant because I knew I had to have something to hold him. I was afraid I would gain so much weight before the wedding that the wedding would be called off.

"My pregnancy was stressful because of my weight. All I gained was twenty-four pounds, which was not a lot of weight, but doctors were pretty strict then. Obviously, fear took over. I remember at the six week checkup, the doctor patted me on the fanny and said 'too much.'

"The reason I went on my second diet was that the man who was the first to give me up, causing me to marry on the rebound, was back in my life. I did the whole thing again. For five minutes, I weighed 134½ pounds. It's marked on a calendar. I keep all my calendars, I'm so obsessed. Then over an eight-year period, I was up to 257 pounds."

Eager to begin my new career, I searched for the job that would open the door. Several interviews later, I had no job, but I did get some advice. "You'll never make it in the fashion world unless you lose some weight." My weight stood in the way again. In desperation, I went to an employment agency hoping to get a job as a secretary. The huge woman behind the desk looked at my application and commented coldly, "Honey, it'll be a lot easier to place you if you lose a couple of pounds." I was furious. What did being plump have to do with typing and filing?

I found a depressing job as a secretary in a convalescent home. I hated it. I was fired just before Christmas. I really felt like a fat failure. I had never been fired before. I collected unemployment and food stamps and I moped. Once again, food became my best friend. After a few months of retreating from the world, I decided I'd better make a major change before it was too late.

I moved to the San Francisco Bay area, found a job in a fabric store, and learned the interior decorating side of fabric sales. On my minimum wage, I could barely afford food and gas. If it hadn't been for my boyfriend, I might have starved. I lost thirty pounds.

It quickly became obvious that I wasn't going anywhere, so I swallowed my pride and went back home to finish school. The life of a home economics teacher looked pretty good by comparison. I threw myself into my studies. I wanted to be the perfect teacher. My weight stayed about the same until the last week of my second semester. I was walking by the school library in the middle of the day when a man attacked me. He meant to rape me. He had some crazy idea that I had led him on; but I didn't even know him. The self-defense class I had taken that semester came in handy. I managed to get away.

The attempted rape changed my life dramatically. I was afraid for men to look at me. I became self-conscious about looking attractive. I started to slowly gain weight again. It wasn't fair—society taught me to invest in my appearance, and now some nut made me doubt my investment. I couldn't maintain a stable weight. I alternately binged and starved.

I remarried and during the next year, I commuted sixty miles each way to school. I finished my undergraduate degree in home economics. Despite the horror stories you hear about student teaching, you're never prepared for the apathy and insolence of your students. After two semesters of teaching, I quit, and once again I felt like a failure.

That summer of 1976 I isolated myself in our little apartment and watched the Bicentennial celebration. I binged and tried to be the textbook homemaker. As my weight went up, my self-esteem went down. I crawled back to Weight Watchers, thinking it was my last chance. I became religious in my quest to lose weight. I was "legal" every week. Though I had my husband's entire family over for Thanksgiving, I stayed legal. I even lost ½ pound that week! Then I had my first, last, and only legal Christmas.

My obsession with dieting and thinness made me totally self-absorbed. My whole life depended on what the scale said in the morning. By the time I planned my menu, spent two hours at the gym, cleaned the house, and prepared dinner, the day was over. This wasn't any kind of life for an achievement-oriented person, so in January I went back to work.

I started working part-time at my old job at the fabric store, but I soon switched to full-time. I took over as manager of the pattern and notion department, and was promised a promotion to assistant fashion coordinator, my dream job. They kept delaying my promotion, and my weight slowly crept back up. I felt I was never going to get anywhere. I blamed it on my weight, knowing the job would have been mine immediately if only I were thin and perfect.

I was frustrated since a friend of mine was making rapid progress in her banking career and I figured I was just as smart as she was. I decided to become a bank president. I typed up some resumes, took a day off, and made the rounds of the local banks. As a lark, I stopped at a rival fabric store to see if they had any positions available. When the manager said they might be looking for a fashion coordinator, my heart stopped.

I was determined to get the job. I wanted it more than anything, I was also afraid. The interview went well, but for two days I held my breath. When I was offered the job, I panicked. What if I couldn't do it? What if they found out I was really a fat person? Who ever heard of a fat fashion coordinator?

Discovery

Because I was scared, I worked ten to twelve hours every day. I began getting up in the middle of the night to work. The business lunches and restaurant dinners pushed my weight up again. I was doing a good job; so I didn't think it would matter. I was shocked when one of the less fashionable store managers told me privately that the other managers didn't think I looked much like a fashion coordinator. What did they want? A clothes horse or a hardworking public relations person? I was furious and scared, but I didn't say anything.

I was in charge of producing a holiday fashion show with the Academy Award-winning designer Edith Head. Why worry about a few pounds when I could work with a star? The show was so good that even Edith Head was impressed. I had been working so hard that I developed pneumonia. While I was home recovering, the truth had caught up with me. No one wants a fat fashion coordinator. I started a crash diet as soon as I went back to work. That was the biggest mistake of my life.

I lost twenty pounds in two weeks. The combination of a lowered resistance, rapid weight loss, and overwork was too much for my system. My hair fell out, my fingernails wouldn't grow and I lost interest in life. Even though this was the job of a lifetime, I could barely force myself out of bed in the morning. The more I tried to diet, the more depressed I became. Everyone was pleased with my new image, but I didn't care. People were wrong to place so much emphasis on body size. I knew they were wrong, and I hated myself for playing their game. I convinced the store owners to host a special fashion show for large ladies. They weren't thrilled by the idea, but they let me try. The response was disappointing. I guess the idea was just too new. My large lady fashion show was held several months before the first issue of *Big Beautiful Woman* magazine appeared. I was miserable. How could people be so narrow-minded? What did body size have to do with a person's abilities. Everyone I knew was always dieting. It was insane.

My husband was worried. He repeatedly tried to talk me into quitting my job. He suggested I start my own business. He pointed out that if I could make money for other people, I could do it for myself. Either he said it enough times or I was too tired to care, because I overcame my fears of losing everything I had dreamed of, and I quietly handed in my resignation. My bosses were shocked. They offered me more money. I felt wonderful. For the first time in my life, I quit while I was ahead.

The exhilaration was shortlived. I was faced with empty days once again. Worst of all after having been "somebody," without a job, I felt like "nobody." I was suffering from job burnout and an identity crisis. I hid. I stopped answering my phone. I only went out only when absolutely necessary.

I gained more weight than ever before. My beautiful clothes no longer fit. I vowed not to buy anymore clothes until I could fit into the old ones. I stopped taking care of myself. I binged all day long. I decided I wouldn't diet until I knew it was for the last time. I was tired of the struggle. I didn't care how I looked or what people thought. I gave up.

After several weeks of total isolation, I started to come alive again. I planted a vegetable garden, bought a pair of roller skates, took acting lessons, and found two things that changed my life.

It sounds overdramatic to credit a book and a magazine with changing my life, but they did. When I saw *Big Beautiful Woman* for the first time, I was both attracted and repelled by a magazine telling its readers that fat is okay. I was embarrassed. By looking at the magazine, I was calling attention to the fact that I was a freak. I bought my copy from the fattest sales clerk in the store. I knew the magazine was right in saying big women were beautiful, but years of social conditioning made it hard for me to accept. I clung to the old-fashioned rules the magazine tried to break. I joked with my husband about how sick the idea was. I didn't want to admit that I couldn't wait for the next issue.

A couple of weeks later, I found *Fat is a Feminist Issue.* I am a feminist, I was puzzled. Feminists aren't supposed to be concerned with looks, and yet a feminist is saying that fat should concern other feminists. I was intrigued.

It seemed like more than a coincidence that in just two weeks I had found two publications that were taking a non-traditional approach to fat. I read the whole book in one night. Finally, someone was saying things I always knew were true. The author talked openly about a subject I had never talked about with anyone, except my best friend, who also had a weight problem. Compulsive eating was coming out of the closet.

I had always known that conventional diets weren't the answer to permanent weight loss. I kept dieting because I didn't know what else to do. At first, I was afraid to follow the book's simple advice. Removing food from the center of your life seemed the logical way to overcome compulsive eating. I was afraid if I followed the book's recommendations and stopped dieting I would start eating and never be able to stop. I had visions of me, in a size 60 dress, not even able to sit up.

I toyed with the book's advice to stop dieting and learn to enjoy eating freely. Everyday I tried to unlearn all the years of diet taboos. I began to allow myself to eat whatever I wanted, as much as I wanted, until I was physically full. It was hard at first. I used the book as an excuse to binge. I went through cycles of craving certain kinds of food. I slowly became aware that my body could tell me when I was physically hungry and when it was satified.

I stopped sneaking food. My husband and I began to talk about my compulsive eating problem, and we talked about what body size meant to us. Gradually, over the course of months of working on it everyday, I stopped compulsive eating. My weight went up, then down, and then it stabilized. This was a first. I was never hungry, except when I really wanted food. I never felt deprived. I achieved a victory—I was no longer a compulsive eater. I was in control. I no longer feared food. Food was no longer the center of my life.

My new weight was higher than it had ever been before. My body was telling me that I should be a big woman. The first truth about fat is that body size and food consumption are separate issues. The second truth about fat is that your attitude and self-image, not your body size, determine how people react to you. If you want to rid yourself of fatphobia, stop giving fat the power that belongs to you. Stop eating compulsively and seize control of your life. Accept your body size, which may mean changing your attitude and self-image. *Big & Beautiful* will show you how to take these four important steps.

More than a year of study, research, growth have gone into the writing of *Big & Beautiful.* The pieces don't fit together overnight, but speed isn't the important factor in this struggle. After all, look at how much time we devote to dieting. Your potential is what's important. Fat Americans have been driven to lives of limited participation by discrimination and exclusion. A wasted life is an irreplaceable resource. I can't think of a single person who has been remembered just because they were thin, except maybe Twiggy. History celebrates doers, not lookers. This book was written to free all of us big, wonderful people from the oppression of a media campaign. We have the right to live full, productive, interesting lives.

Read on and learn why we suffer from fatphobia. Examine the new research on nutrition, metabolism, and genetics. Arm yourself with a knowledge of the historical trends in body fashion. Discover how highly profitable media hype helps make you a second-class citizen. Learn how to battle the stereotypes that limit you. Most of all, learn to love yourself for the unique contribution you can make, whether you are fat or thin. If *Big & Beautiful* accomplishes nothing else, let it at least give you comfort of knowing you are not alone and that you are not a freak.

ONWARD TO A RAISED CONSCIOUSNESS AND A NEW WORLD.

Chapter 2

FREEDOM FROM FATPHOBIA

F atphobia. Cute. I wonder what it really means. It's probably just another one of those whacky diet books. I can't face another diet. Dieting just isn't worth it. I can never keep the weight off. Well, why not? I've tried everything else...."

FREEDOM FROM COMPULSIVE EATING

I tried everything, too. I thought I was crazy—why did a little fat mean so much? Why couldn't I just lose weight and keep it off? There must be something wrong with me. I was a fat compulsive eater, and I was a thin compulsive eater. I honestly couldn't remember a time when I wasn't fat or dieting. If I didn't hate myself for being fat, I hated the world because I thought it wouldn't let me eat. I dieted and binged, binged and dieted, and then one day, I stopped.

I stopped dieting. I braced myself for the wave of fat that would engulf me. I ate nervously and waited. I ate and ate and ate. I ate all the things I had been denying myself. I gained some weight, but not nearly as much as I thought I would. I was still human. The more I gave myself permission to enjoy food, the less I needed to overeat. I stopped eating compulsively. I stopped bingeing. I started enjoying food, really enjoying it. I started enjoying life, too.

CAN YOU BE FAT AND HAPPY?

You're probably thinking, "Okay, so you gave up. You're still fat. You can't really be fat and happy in a world that worships being thin. People expect you to always be on a diet. Diets are 'in.' Fat people are foodaholics, out of control. They have to be restrained for their own good."

I used to believe the stereotypes. You're not supposed to be happy and successful unless you're tall, thin, and young. The stereotypes are promoted by forces that have a big economic stake in making us believe fat is more than a difference in physical size. No wonder it's hard to see the truth. We have to be realistic. People do judge us by our appearance. But that doesn't mean we have to limit ourselves to fat clothes, fat jobs, and fat personalities. We can learn how to deal with fat as a highly stigmatized characteristic in our culture. We can change the meaning of fat for ourselves and for others.

We know the fat stereotypes aren't true. Fat people aren't jollier, anti-social, or anti-sex. Most of us have quietly endured the nasty cracks and embarrassing moments because we didn't want to cause a scene. We've tried being gracious and tolerant, but some people just don't seem to understand or care.

OUTSIDE FORCES LIMIT OUR POTENTIAL

We have a lot to unlearn. We can't let outside forces limit our potential. The media, our friends, and our families have defined our lives for too long. It's time for us to take charge. We must learn to speak up. After all, the difference between fat people and thin people is a matter only of inches.

If you're nodding your head, then you know what fatphobia is. It isn't a scientific term. Fatphobia's a term I coined to describe the unrealistic fear and hatred of being fat. Fatphobia exists because we let it exist. Two image problems contribute to fatphobia. First, we are all supposed to be the superwomen—thin, attractive, well-dressed, in control, successful, and loved. The superwoman is everything we want, and she doesn't exist. But we still try to measure up. We start really believing two pounds or one half inch is going to make the difference. We lose sight of what's acceptable and realistically obtainable.

Jeri's Story

Jeri, a bright and articulate young woman, explains how the superwoman image has impeded her career.

"If you try to change the world, you place yourself in double jeopardy. You can't be an achiever unless you fit the stereotype. For instance, I'd like to be successful in advertising, but I couldn't play the game the way they play it—being super thin, dressing to kill. I feel that I would not be acceptable in that arena. I don't feel I could compete based on my talents alone. No, I mean based on my looks. In other words, my talents don't matter."

We forget the superwoman we see in the ads is a model who makes a full-time job out of looking good. She's 5'10", ten years younger, and forty pounds lighter than we are, but we still compare. We paint and massage, lotion and diet, and she still looks younger every year.

We see her playing volleyball on the beach with gorgeous men, while we scrub the toilet. She dances all night, while we punch a time clock. No wonder we keep looking for that wonder diet that's going to make it happen for us. Unfortunately, even if you do get thin, you still have to scrub toilets and punch a time clock. I've made the trip several times. That is, my body made the trip, but my mind never seemed to make the transition. My body would become thin but I would still be the same fat lady in my head. All the problems that I had attributed to being fat were still there. I had achieved the physical image but my self-image hadn't changed.

No one wants life to be a commercial, where everyone has perfect teeth and shiny hair. But we'd all like our lives to be better. If you've been a little bored lately, or you feel a little out of control, you go on a diet—the magic cure. A diet can make everything seem better.

Every Monday, we start with new dedication. You're so good that by Wednesday you've lost three pounds. Three pounds less and you're a new woman. You feel better, you look better, you swear you have more energy. You're in control. Being thin is great. You've worked so hard that a thin, sexy person like you deserves a little reward. Somehow the reward gets out of hand and the next thing you know, it's Monday again. We keep kidding ourselves until losing three pounds doesn't do it anymore. Then what? You diet harder?

It's not the three pounds. It's not diets or being thin. We're hooked on the process. Dieting means caring. Dieting gives us a reason to care. What happens when you diet? You start spending more time on your hair and makeup. You may even buy some new clothes. You smile more. People start noticing. We think it's because of the diet. We diet because it makes us feel good, in control. It gives us permission to be human.

What people notice is not the lost weight but the attention you're giving yourself, the effort, the confidence you are showing. They're responding to the real you. Diets give us confidence to be ourselves. But it's a fragile confidence, and it depends on the number that registers on the scale each morning. Diets give you the boost a department store makeup demonstration can. A new face can make you feel like a different person. But the new packaging doesn't express the inner you, and it's gone when you wash your face.

I don't know why we need an excuse to care about ourselves when we're fat. When I was fat, I always felt it was a waste to invest in nice things. When I did buy something new, it was from the bargain basement with little fit or style. Why shop when all you can find are fat lady costumes? I felt I didn't deserve to look nice. My closet was filled with cute size seven through fourteens that never wore out because I never stayed thin long enough. The bigger the size, the duller the clothes. I vowed never to buy anything new until I lost weight. Sound familiar? We think we're just fat temporarily.

This kind of fatphobic thinking limits us. We begin to believe fatphobia stereotypes like fat people prefer jobs out of the public eye, fat people don't care how they look, fat people wish they were thin, fat people are jolly to hide the fact that they hate themselves. So how do we prove these deeply ingrained assumptions aren't true? Almost everyone believes fat is bad, so how do we convince them otherwise? Can we? You bet we can. We're going to use the tricks of professional image-makers to free ourselves from fatphobia.

Projecting an image is a way of communicating. According to some experts, as much as 90 percent of our communication is nonverbal. We're going to make sure our nonverbal signals tell the world that big is beautiful. The kind of image we're going to work on takes personality, attitude, identity, posture, movement, mannerisms, lifestyle, goals, and grooming into consideration. After we inventory these things, we can create a package that says it all.

START BY BELIEVING IN YOURSELF

Successful image development depends on accepting certain premises. Before you can change your image, you have to start believing in yourself. First, you have to believe you have good taste. Sometimes we can distort our good taste by listening to other people. Second, you have to believe it is okay to like yourself, even if you're not perfect. That includes wanting to look your best. It's normal to care, no matter what size the package. And third, most people need some help forming an objective view of themselves.

You may need some help in developing your new image. You can pay a fancy image consultant for their expert eye and unfailing good taste, or you can learn to do it yourself. Even if you do consult an image-maker for help and support, you still need to be sure you're getting your money's worth. As a professional image consultant, my main goal has been to develop a self-help system to free people from fatphobia. We can change the world by changing ourselves.

A recent Celanese Corporation study showed the sale of large size clothing doubled from 1974 to 1978. The market has gone crazy since then. It's the beginning of a whole new era in women's fashions. Another study predicts this trend will produce a wider variety of clothing styles and sizes to fit other groups of women with special needs. We already see more large size clothing on the market. The industry is also recognizing the petite woman's needs. With a little prodding, we can get them to pay attention to the tall big woman and the young big woman. When we stop wasting our breath apologizing for being different and start demanding what we want, there'll be lots of people listening.

NAAFA: FAT POWER

The big-is-beautiful movement isn't new. The National Association to Aid Fat Americans (NAAFA) has been around since 1969 trying to get us to use our economic and political strength to change public opinion. It's taken ten years and a special person like Carole Shaw, editor of *Big Beautiful Woman Magazine,* to get anyone to take big women seriously. Perhaps the big is beautiful idea is finally catching on because the younger generation of women who have been exposed to the women's movement won't accept the prejudice. It could be the result of a backlash of the organic/health craze. Whatever the reason, a new world that is free from fatphobia is at our doorstep.

Before you rush out with your "Fat Power" sign to picket the nearest weight-loss clinic, let's consider a more effective way to foster this change. The best way for us to change the fatphobia image is by casting the true American ballot at the nearest cash register that provides us with what we want. We have to invest in the new image that is being offered. If we don't show our economic support, manufacturers will lose interest, and we'll be right back where we started. The only chance we have to change attitudes

Freedom

about fat people is to show others we care about how we look. We want to look good. We want to belong. We deserve to be treated like anyone else. Before you get the idea I'm a shill for the fashion industry, I'm not. I just want the large size customer to become a better consumer when it comes to her image. I don't want you to spend any more money than you normally spend. I just want you to become a little more selective.

It doesn't take a lot of money to improve your image. In fact, having a lot of money can hamper image development. If you can afford not to be selective, you may buy on impulse without a plan. You can end up with a closet full of great clothes, a dressing table piled with makeup, and no clear image.

I'll tell you where you can get the cash to improve your image. Let's assume you spend an average of ten dollars a week on diets, diet doctors, gyms, exercise classes, diet books, diet foods, foods you throw away so you won't binge, and food you binge on. That means we spend at least $520 a year on fatphobia. With that same $520, you could get your hair restyled and have a makeup consultation. Before choosing your new wardrobe, you could have your colors analyzed. You could take a class or buy a book. You could take a friend to lunch, and have enough money left over to place an ad for a new Fatphobia Awareness Training (FAT) support group. All these things will do you more good than another diet.

DEVELOPING PERSONAL STYLE

As educated consumers, we shouldn't expect the fashion industry to design individual looks for each of us. In fact, why should we settle for an assembly-line look? We give clothes our personal style. Many women complain no one is making the kind of clothes they want. It's true—there's plenty of room for improvement. If you don't like the fashion news, go out and make some of your own. Don't wait for the industry to package the look you want. Learn the language of fashion. If you speak their language, you can tell the manufacturers you want a black satin teddy with antique French lace. That's going to get more results than saying you want better looking lingerie. Don't rely on the fashion industry to have good taste, after all, they're the ones who gave us Hawaiian-print house dresses. Blessed be the customer who speaks up, for she shall have a better image.

I know—you're thinking, "How can I figure out what I want when I don't know what's possible or right for me?" I'm going to teach you how to recognize your personal style. Once you've found it, you'll never again have to be a slave to fashion's fancies. You're wondering how you get other people to accept the new you. You have to shatter the misconceptions others have about our limitations. Who says we can't be urban cowgirls if we want to be? Who says big women can't be successful businesswomen? You can be anything you want to be. You can be sexy, adventurous, sophisticated. You have to redirect your attitude toward a new goal. Attitude redirection requires focusing your attention and maintaining a steady push toward the new.

We all feel more comfortable around the things we are accustomed to. When we're faced with the challenges created by change, we usually want to retreat to the old and familiar. For instance, when you first notice shoe styles are changing your first reaction is, "I'll never wear those ridiculous, ugly things." You resist change by buying what you're used to, but gradually you see your friends wearing the new style. You still resist, but it's getting harder to find your old style. Pretty soon you notice everyone is wearing the new style, and some of the shoes look pretty good. Your eye is getting used to the change. Finally, you're forced to buy the new style because you can't find any shoes in your old style. Change has occurred but it was so gradual, you hardly noticed it. The same process can work for body size preference. It may take years, but we *can* change today's negative attitudes about fat. The last major body style change occured in the 1920's. Isn't it time for a change?

We'll explore attitude redirection more fully in the next chapter, but you don't have to wait. You can start changing your attitude right now. From this moment on, you will believe you are a worthwhile person with a right to be happy and attractive. You have the right to stop being the victim. You don't have to take abuse.

There is a beautiful woman inside your chubby body. She can't develop unless you let her escape from your prison of doubt. Being thin won't make you beautiful. Thin is a symbol, but it's not the answer. Believing in that beautiful woman may entail a radical shift in your thinking, so give it time. Listen to the facts and let them sink in. This is an evolutionary process, not an overnight miracle.

Low self-esteem hurts, and don't let anyone try to tell you it doesn't. It used to be a constant ache for me. It hurts to feel everyone else is better than you. If you want the pain to go away, you've got to discover the right balance between your body image, your attitude, and your compulsive eating. Don't expect perfection, especially by next weekend's class reunion. If you're in too much of a hurry, you'll miss all the rewards self-improvement can bring. Getting there is half the fun. Nice things will happen to you on the way to learning self-respect.

That doesn't mean if you get a new hairstyle, you'll return home to find Superman in your bed. It takes time. What have you got to lose? If you've tried everything else, why not try a big dose of self-respect.

Working on your outward image first will give you an immediate ego boost. Looking better always makes you feel better. But don't forget that your outward image has to reflect the inner person, or you'll seem phony. Read the next few chapters; have fun experimenting with new looks. Fashion is supposed to be fun. Changes in fashion add spice to our lives. Then after you've gained a little confidence, take yourself one step further from fatphobia. Work on your attitude in the Fatphobia Awareness Training (FAT) support groups described in the last chapter.

Learn first to develop a personal style. Learn how to use color to build a great wardrobe inexpensively. Learn to be a wise shopper, to select the right services, determine quality, and enhance your personality areas by paying attention to details like makeup and accessories. I'll show you how to apply universal principles of design to make the most of your body. Along the way, you'll find out how to use your economic clout to win respect and recognition. You're going to learn how to become a big beautiful person that no one will want to ignore.

Later, you'll learn a technique that will help you understand where fat-phobia came from and how you can be permanently free from its oppression. You'll learn how to deal with the painful subject of compulsive eating and to control it and, thus, control our lives.

Start thinking about friends who might share the exercises suggested in the next few chapters. Many fat people tend to withdraw, and isolation can magnify any problem. FAT Groups aren't therapy groups. FAT groups won't solve all your problems, but they will help you grow by increasing your awareness and providing support which can be pretty scary at times.

After you've enjoyed *Big & Beautiful* for the first time, I hope you will continue your personal growth by reading the book again. Image development is a never-ending process. The better you feel about yourself, the better you'll want your image to be. Instead of a vicious downward cycle of diet, failure, and self-hatred, start an upward growth cycle that will bring you the satisfaction a diet never could.

We've got a lot of work to do, so let's get started.

Big &
Beautiful

Photo courtesy of Lane Bryant.

Chapter 3

WHERE DO YOU START: ATTITUDE

What's hot and what's not in image:

Casual chic is hot,
Sloppy is not.

Recycling, torn, baggy pantyhose to prop up tomato plants is hot,
wearing them is not.

Finding a great buy is hot,
Impulsive buying is not.

Predicting your future fashion needs is hot,
Following the crowds is not.

Polyester that looks like silk is hot,
Polyester that looks like polyester is not.

WHAT'S HOT AND WHAT'S NOT

Who cares what's hot and what's not in image? We should since we are combatting a negative media campaign. But we're not the only people concerned with image. After the "do your own thing" image free-for-all in the seventies, a lot of people are looking for some direction. At a career day seminar a few months ago, I spoke to a group of college students about the importance of image in business. One student asked if image was really that important. She pointed out that members of her generation had the benefit of self-help courses, and she felt she and her peers were above such ego-centered, archaic indulgences.

I replied that with all the advances made by the personal growth-human potential movement, we should be able to sell ourselves without worrying about our appearance. You'd think we would be able to see the wonderful person inside everyone. I tested this supposition by posing a question. "Suppose you're the president of a Fortune 500 company looking for your successor. Would you hire someone who showed up for the interview with a broken zipper, a run in her nylons, and greasy fingerprints on her resume?" This got a chuckle from the audience, but I made my point. The image we present is important. Your image could be the deciding factor in your success. The shift in politics and attitudes indicates the image we project will be even more important in the future. Mass marketing techniques are making us a nation of look alikes. The problem of the eighties isn't going to be how to fit in, but how to stand out. We can thank the media revolution for making us image gourmets. We have had hours of practice judging hundreds of people, products, and services. We've become visual connoisseurs. Now we must turn our gourmet eye to ourselves. Image is going to be important whether you're on your way up the corporate ladder or you're trying to find Mr. Right.

Recently, there has been a spate of books and articles about dressing for success and looking beautiful. Some of the authors have tried to address the problems faced by big women. What makes this book different from all the others? I'm interested in helping you find an image that fits your personality, and not just your body dimensions. The traditional approach places too much emphasis on figure flaws. Instead of hiding your problems, I want you to emphasize your assets. In addition, I want to examine all the issues—social, emotional, and physical—facing big women.

Terri's Story

Negative attitudes about fat affect our lives in serious ways. Terri's words illustrate just how harmful these attitudes, our own and those of others, can be. "The way I feel about my body changes by the hour. When things aren't going well and I don't feel good about myself, I see fat that isn't there. I still get dissatisfied with this body, with legs that are too big for somebody's standard of what legs should look like. I am very self-conscious. I still don't wear skirts very often, and that's after losing 120 pounds."

Louise's Story

Louise is another woman who has found her low self-image is holding her back in her career. "I think being fat affects me psychologically more than anything else. I'm in sales, and I have to be very outgoing. This terrifies me. I'm probably in the wrong field. Often I'll go out with a client, and I'll just bomb out. I sit back and think, 'Is it because I'm fat?'

"This morning I had to get up at a broker's meeting and make a presentation. It scared the living hell out of me. These people are my peers, the people I work with. I shouldn't be afraid of them. But I feel like they're sitting there looking at me thinking, 'Why is she so fat? Why doesn't she do something to help herself?' I think being fat holds me back more in my mind. There will always be people who won't deal with me because I'm fat. But some people won't deal with someone who's a minority, or who has freckles, or whatever. I've always felt that if I were nice and slender, I would be much more successful than I am."

A letter in Dr. Joyce Brothers' column sums up the problems negative attitudes towards fat people can create. The writer complained that she and her husband stopped making love because she was fat. She was desperate. The good doctor advised her to lose a few pounds, even though Dr. Brothers doubted fat was the real problem. If fat wasn't the real problem, why did Dr. Brothers advise the woman to lose weight? Why didn't she explain the problem was what the weight represented. The writer needed help, not a pat answer. Dr. Brothers' response reflects a negative attitude that is shared by thousands of others.

Another woman in one of my Fatphobia Awareness Training (FAT) groups confessed that she and her husband had a similiar problem. She was a beautiful blonde with perfect makeup, lovely clothes, an ample hourglass figure, and long, manicured nails. She was a desirable woman, but, because of her husband's attitude problem, no longer felt she was desirable. Instead, she felt worthless. Because of her husband's indifference, she didn't believe any man would find her attractive.

A fellow member of the group shared her solution to a related problem. This woman was a large, gorgeous, exotic lady. After taking years of verbal abuse from her husband, she finally told him that while she might not be a raving beauty, he was far from the ideal of male perfection. She told him, "When I look at you objectively, I see a short, bald, skinny, bow-legged man with a crooked nose. When I look at you through the eyes of love, I see the most glamorous, sexy, virile, wonderful man I've ever known. Now which way do you want me to look at you? He said, 'Through the eyes of love.' He has never said another unkind word about my size. That was the turning point in my husband's attitude."

A woman in another group had a different approach to changing negative attitudes about fat people. For years, she had struggled to be a super-woman. She finally told her husband, "I'm going to go to bed with every man in San Jose if that's what it takes to prove I'm still a desirable woman!" She didn't even get the chance to flirt. The thought of someone else making love to his wife was enough to make him change his attitude and his behavior.

Often all it takes to change a relationship is a change in attitude. These women changed their images of themselves, and that helped change the attitude of those around them. We tell people how they should treat us by the image we project. Your appearance, or image, will reflect your low self-esteem, and people will treat you accordingly.

I can also speak from my own experience. Fatphobia has hurt me. I almost got a divorce because of my poor self-image. My husband hasn't always appreciated the sensuous curves of my big body. I lost thirty pounds just so he would marry me. We battled about my weight for seven years. Every time I lost weight, he thought the problem was over. He couldn't understand why I would gain weight back when I had such a hard time taking it off. He began to doubt my sanity, among other things. As the years went by, our fights became more serious. I began to think I was too fat to be loved. I couldn't love myself enough to stay thin, so why should anyone else love me?

The more depressed I became about my weight, the less attention I paid to my appearance. I stopped looking at clothes, putting on makeup, shaving my legs, brushing my teeth, or washing my hair. I totally lost interest in myself. The moment of truth arrived. All my clothes either wore out or became too small. I either had to lose weight, buy new clothes, or join a nudist colony. I moped around the house, unsure of what to do. I finally went shopping because I didn't have anything to wear to a party we'd been invited to. Even if I crash dieted, I couldn't have lost enough weight to fit into anything I owned. I was very depressed.

So, I found myself at the local shopping mall looking at some nice, safe jeans and a loose polyester top. I really felt that I didn't deserve to look good. I walked by the rack of sale dresses and there was the same dress I'd seen on a skinny model in *Vogue*. It was a bright robin's egg blue. I couldn't resist. That dress stirred feelings I thought were long dead. I couldn't wait to try it on.

The material was so light and gauzy, I felt naked. I twirled in front of the mirror. I loved it, but did I dare buy it? I tried the belt on, hoping it would ruin the look and I could go back to my nice, safe clothes. The dress looked even better. I cautiously opened the dressing room door in search of a three-way mirror. I was half-hoping someone would notice me, and boy, did they. I felt like a model. With such a positive response, I almost broke my arm getting my credit card out to pay for the dress.

I went home, showered, shaved, primped, and pampered myself as I hadn't done in months. When my husband arrived, the look he gave me was worth the price of the dress. I hadn't seen that look in a long time. Needless to say, we had a great evening. Late that night, after a romantic interlude, we were finally able to talk—after all those years of shouting, tears, and pain. We had never discovered the root of our problem because we were blaming my weight and not our attitudes about it.

My husband wanted me to look good; he didn't necessarily want me to be thin. We both had assumed that if I were thin I'd look good, and in the past, the only time I did look and feel good was when I was thin. That false assumption almost caused us to get a divorce. Once I started paying attention to myself, we discovered the problem wasn't my size. Instead of dreaming of the person I wanted to become, I started being that person. I stopped waiting and started living.

When I bought that dress I wasn't playing it safe anymore. By taking a risk I learned I could shape people's attitudes about me. I didn't have to hide my personality because of a stereotype. When I bought that dress, I stopped trying to hide the fact that I was fat. I accepted responsibility for the way people reacted to me. You know what? I haven't heard a single negative comment about my size or my eating habits since that day.

I'm not going to kid you by saying the blue dress was the solution to all my problems. But it did introduce me to a new way of thinking. My husband and I started communicating instead of fighting. We found he wanted to be proud of his wife. We both can see that it's alright to dream and fantasize, but we are also realistic. As long as I like and take care of myself, he'll be proud of me. He still finds most thin women attractive, but the other day he said he thought a certain model in a commercial was too thin to be sexy. We both laughed. He never thought he'd say any woman could be too thin.

My experiences made me wonder where I got the idea that I couldn't be both fat and attractive. After much soul searching, I discovered negative attitudes stemmed from humiliating trips to the chubbette shop. I used to long for the fluffy pink Easter dresses in the regular girls' section. I remember whining, "Why can't I have one like this? Why doesn't it ever come in my size?" My mother always answered, "Because you're too fat." Too fat for what? Too fat to be human? What had I done wrong? Why were they punishing me because I was fat? Years later, I was still punishing myself. The hurt and humiliation I experienced as a child were with me as an adult.

The process of developing attitudes is complex. I remember my grandmother lived with us while I was growing up. She was an attractive, well-put-together, big lady with great style. She took pity on her chubby granddaughter, as she had with her daughter. She couldn't stand the tantrums and heartbreak these shopping trips caused. My family was a working class family, and my parents couldn't afford to spend a lot of money on little girl's dresses. So my grandmother drafted patterns on newspaper to make me those fluffy pink dresses. I may have had to endure my younger brother's hand-me-down flannel shirts and jeans during the week, but on Sunday I looked like a princess. When I had on my stiff petticoat and patent leather shoes with taps, I felt just as pretty as any other little girl. For an hour every week I could forget I was a four-eyed fat freak.

To change your attitude, you've got to explore your experiences and prejudices. All your experiences, both negative and postive, shape your attitudes. Once you understand why you feel as you do about being fat, don't expect an instant revolution. You've got to learn to respect yourself. Be patient with yourself, but don't let that patience become inertia. It's up to you to break out of the fatphobia trap.

PEOPLE CAN DETECT A POOR SELF-IMAGE

Image and attitude are so closely related that it is hard to study them separately. Your self-image, or the way you see yourself, is usually the way other people perceive you. If you sneak into a room clutching your coat around you and sink into a seat in the back of the room, you're telegraphing your lack of confidence. If you march proudly down the center aisle and take a seat in the front row, you're telling people what a grand lady you are.

A poor self-image can be hard to change. You don't like yourself, so you concentrate on your faults, hoping to improve. You become so obsessed with your faults that you overlook your virtues. It's the old self-fulfilling prophecy—if you think you can be attractive, healthy, and happy, chances are you will be, if you believe life is beyond your control, it may well be. Where do you want to focus your energy? You can't hang beautiful clothes on a person and expect an instant transformation. The clothes won't shine unless you do.

Your body image is a physical expression of your attitude. How you feel about your body affects how you wear your clothes. Poor body image may be the biggest problem we must overcome. The success of your image development depends on your acceptance of your body, right now, the way it is. I know I've said it before, but we still have a lot of body size prejudices to unlearn. I can't stress enough how irrelevant size is to looking good.

GETTING ACQUAINTED WITH YOUR BODY

Let's work on getting acquainted with your body. You can't accept something you aren't familiar with. Most fat women tend to focus on their faces or minds as representative of their personality. Margaret's comments are typical of fat women who are alienated from their bodies.

"I won't look at myself in a full-length mirror. I look from the neck up. I can accept myself from the neck up because I can fiddle with my hair or something. But when you try on clothes, you can't run from the mirror. I look at my body and think, 'That can't be me. It's someone else's body.' It just doesn't sink in to me that it's me."

I used to hate full-length mirrors, especially the rear view. I found the easiest way to overcome my body prejudice and focus on reality was to make myself into a work of art. I went to my husband and told him I wanted to take some pictures of myself from all angles. He was delighted to help. I changed into my leotard and tights. When I entered the room, he fell on the floor laughing. He wanted to know if I was the unknown fat person. I'd walked into the room with a paper bag over my head, reasoning that if I considered my face to represent my real self I'd have to cover it up to get a more objective opinion of who I am. After we stopped laughing, my husband photographed me from all sides. If you don't have a partner who's fun-loving enough to assist you in this exercise, a three-way mirror will do. I liked having the pictures because I could tape them on the closet door. When I dressed in the morning, they were a gentle reminder of what I had to work with. Those silly pictures have helped me learn to accept my body.

I invented another experiment to prove that body size is relative. I went to a dime store and bought a cheap ring two sizes too large. I wore it around the house for a couple of days, and I reminded myself I could be big enough to fit that ring. But even if it fit, I would still be the same person. It was a way of focusing my attention on how unimportant body size really is. There were people who wore that ring size, but just because their hands were bigger than mine did not mean they were better or worse than I was. I then applied the same reasoning to my image.

I hope you try these exercises. They will help you get in touch with your feelings about body size. Attitude is one of those things that can best be dealt with when you have someone to give you support and feedback. In this last chapter, I will describe how to organize a FAT support group. In the meantime, find a friend or two to get you started now. You need the objective opinions a couple of good friends can give you. We're not trying to be amateur psychiatrists. We're just trying to gain a better understanding of a complex problem. I recommend you limit your sharing to one friend, two at the most. Until you are accustomed to the group process, too many opinions can be confusing. Give yourself time to find out who you are before you try working in a big group. Make sure the friends you choose are people you trust and whose opinions you respect. These friends don't have to be fat. There are plenty of fat people inside skinny bodies.

Plan a lunch or dinner party where you and your friends can be alone. Talk about how you feel about your body size. Discuss where these feelings came from. Do the exercises I've suggested. Remember, sharing is caring.

Photo courtesy of YOUNG STUFF a division of Stout Sportswear Group.

Chapter 4

THE LANGUAGE OF IMAGE

Go to a public place and do some creative people watching. Try to identify what each person's image says to you. Accompany me on an imaginary trip to a restaurant and see how it's done. We're going to borrow a technique that psychic entertainers, such as fortune tellers, use to gather information about a client. It's a highly refined form of people watching called cold reading.

A sidewalk cafe is perfect for our assignment. We can sit here and enjoy a cup of coffee and a piece of chocolate pie, and no one will suspect our true mission. Here comes a likely candidate. Enter Madam X. She is wearing a skirt, soft blouse, and a blazer. Nice jacket, but her shoes are wrong. She pauses at the door and looks around the room. Madam X walks confidently to a group of people deep in conversation. She smiles and joins their conversation.

What have we learned so far, besides the fact that they have great pie here? Madam X looks like a businesswoman who's meeting people for lunch. I'd say she's well liked by the group. If the group had fallen silent or disbanded, I wouldn't have made that assumption. Madam X comes across as confident and well-put-together, so I'd say she's successful. Her shoes don't match the rest of her outfit, which probably means she's on her feet all day and wears them for comfort, not fashion.

Let's order another cup of coffee before taking a closer look. Madam X is wearing a rather plain wedding band. This could mean she either likes simple jewelry or she wants people to think she's unavailable. Her hair and makeup are simple, indicating she's not overly concerned about elaborate grooming.

They've ordered drinks. Madam X is playing with the ice in her glass. Her body language says she's bored or uncomfortable or both. She's probably in direct sales and trapped at a boring business lunch.

Now you try it. Be crazy. Be creative. Who's going to know? It's a good way to sharpen your powers of observation.

It's your turn. What can you tell me about Madam H., the center of the commotion at the door. You can't help but notice her energetic twins who are amusing themselves by trying to climb out of their strollers. Madam H. turns in time to catch the salt shaker her four year old has knocked off the neighboring table.

Considering the circumstances, Madam H's denim skirt and cotton tee-shirt accented with grape juice stain appropriate. Her hair and makeup are attractive, despite the chaos around her. Madam H. gives the impression of a confident mother on a typical shopping trip.

What did you learn? After some practice, you'll become aware of how much self-image is conveyed in physical ways. You'll find people are easy to "read" once you know what to look for. You'd be amazed how accurate cold reading can be at times. If we're so good at reading other people's image messages, why don't we naturally send the right message? Because, no one has ever taught us how to analyze our body language. We can learn to read other people's image messages, but it's far more difficult to practice on yourself. Try this exercise in the privacy of your bathroom or bedroom. It will help you improve your expressiveness. Close your eyes and think of an emotion. With your eyes still closed, try to express that emotion with

Image

your face. Open your eyes and look in the mirror. Were you successful? Practice this exercise once each morning, and your ability to communicate will increase dramatically.

Part of the problem is our lack of objectivity, but most of what holds us back is the problem of the "shoulds" and "oughts." What if we try something different and people laugh? People might not understand if you don't look the way fat people are supposed to look. It's as though we can read the language, but we are afraid to speak it. It might help if we define the language of image. We already know attitude and body image are part of this language. The other part is our physical appearance. This physical image doesn't exist until we create it. Take away hair, makeup, and clothes and all you have is a naked body. Your physical image should be used to create a mystique, a mood, or an identity.

What goes into creating a physical image? Hair, clothes, and makeup form a foundation. Also important are voice, movement, grooming, body language, and the way you wear the clothes. If you can see it, it's part of your physical image. Let's divide the physical image into the sections—face and hair, posture, voice, body language, and physical condition—so you can better evaluate your image.

ABOVE THE NECK

Your face and hair are your most important personality areas. You can communicate subtle image messages with your face. Is your face as expressive as it could be? Do you use your face to convey emotions? Watch people in commercials. Observe how they use their faces to tell the story. Their expressions don't usually come naturally. Actors spend hours studying their expressions in front of a mirror.

Eye contact is also important. Looking people directly in the eye shows them you are in control. Direct eye contact indicates confidence. Eye contact and a firm handshake are especially important for women. It conveys assertiveness, which is something women should learn more about.

Makeup and hairstyles date you more quickly than anything except hat styles. Remember all that money you're going to save by not going on crazy diets? This is one of the places to spend it. Read the beauty tips in magazines. Try new products. Your face and hair should be two of your most treasured assets. Every so often, I splurge on a makeover. I have the works—new hair style, facial, manicure, new makeup. Not only does it do wonders for my ego, but it gives me a second opinion. You can learn many tricks from professionals, but the first time an expert says something will make me look thinner, I set them straight. Telling them I don't have to look thin to look good usually changes their attitude. Be sure to ask questions. You're paying for their time, so get the most out of it. After they're finished and before I pay the bill, I head for the ladies room. In the privacy of the bathroom, I evaluate what they've done. I may like only one or two things they've tried, but this private evaluation gives me time to prepare for the sales pitch that always comes at the end. If I really like the new shade of lipstick or the way they've made up my eyes, I'll buy the product. If not, the experience of being pampered is worth the price.

Advice from the Experts

Before giving you advice, I consulted experts Jake Politte and Adolfo Voglino, owners of San Francisco's Illusions makeup and hair styling salon. They understand the problems large women have encountered in trying to improve their images. Jake told me about a makeup and hair styling demonstration at Zoftig, the quality boutique for large women here in San Francisco, where one large woman reluctantly volunteered to be Jake's guinea pig. She explained her embarrassment, saying "It's common knowledge that fat ladies shouldn't wear makeup." Jake asked her where that rule came from. Convincing that first volunteer convinced the other women that it was okay for fat ladies to look nice. Although Jake and Adolfo have traveled in the highest fashion circles, their advice is tailored to the real world. Both agree that you should ignore what's being shown in the fashion magazines. According to Adolfo, "There is no trend to be followed by everyone. Wear what suits you. Fads are for teenagers. Hair and makeup have to fit a person's lifestyle.

Jake and Adolfo feel most large woman play it too safe with their image. Too many large women spend too much time worrying about their imagined flaws. Large women should enhance their softness and elegance. There is often something special about the way large women carry themselves. Large women can be sexier than skinny women, if they let themselves.

Adolfo Voglino, a hairstylist for twenty-five years, says, "A lot of women, especially when they are large, are embarrassed. You are what you are. Large women can wear high fashion hair and clothes. It's not what you wear, but how you wear it. Just know your limits."

Adolfo advises large women to look for a hairstylist who has someone that can work with large women, someone with an eye for balance. He advises, "Unless you bring a little self-confidence with you, they'll just take you for your money. If they don't treat you right, to hell with them. A true professional cares about customers, no matter what their size.

I'm particular about my hair. Most big women have nice hair, perhaps because we're well-nourished. If you haven't changed your hairstyle in the last ten years, maybe it's time for a new look. When I'm looking for a new stylist, I ask people I see on the street. They're usually flattered, and are more than happy to share their secret. I don't skimp when it comes to a good cut, because I know it will save me time and it tops off a good image. I'll gladly pay a little more, and I'll even give a large tip to make sure my stylist stays interested in me and my hair.

Adolfo advises, "The most important thing to remember is to keep it simple and have a good cut. If you have dark, full hair, don't get a tight permanent—it doesn't look right. Large women should have lots of hair to balance their larger bodies. I try to talk many large women into growing their hair out. But if you do grow it out, make sure it's not too long. Wear it with style. Keep your hair clean. Since big women often have more oil glands, it's important to keep both hair and skin clean.

"Heat doesn't hurt hair as long as it's not applied for too long. Conditioning too much can be as bad as not conditioning at all, because it doesn't allow the hair to breathe. Change shampoos and conditioners every few months, because any product can form a buildup if it's used for too long. Read the labels before you buy. Some companies actually use lard, acetone, alcohol, and ammonia in their products."

In addition, Adolfo recommends geometric cuts for large women. He says these cuts add drama and interest to the face. "Use the hair to frame the face and neck. The biggest crime large women commit is cutting their hair too short. Don't be afraid to color and highlight your hair. It can really give a tired image a lift."

Jake Politte, a model turned makeup artist, understands the problems facing large women because of his younger sister. "She was always dieting. She would starve herself. She felt she couldn't wear certain clothes." Where makeup is concerned Jake's philosophy is simple, less is more. His program takes from ten to fifteen minutes in the morning. Jake believes that too much makeup can give large women the "Santa Claus syndrome," where the makeup takes over and hides the face.

Jake warns that "too much dieting can damage the skin. Doctors don't tell you what happens after prolonged dieting. Your skin loses it's elasticity. Large women often have the good skin because it has more oil, which keeps it plumped up. At forty, many large women don't even have wrinkles.

"Color is important. I work with skin tone, eyes, and hair color when I select makeup for a woman. I use the face to create a triangular focal point. Think of the eyes, cheeks, and lips forming a triangle. By using color in these areas, you draw attention to the face. The eyes are the most important place to use color, especially at night. Lip and cheek colors help to define the face.

"Be particularly careful when you select your foundation. It should round out your skin tone, not change its color. Orange, and many of the earth tones, give your skin a pulled down look. The chemical content of some foundations causes them to turn orange when applied." Jake recommends you test a foundation color on the chest and neck rather than the arm, and then allow time for this chemical reaction to occur. According to Jake, water-based foundation are less likely than oil-based ones to block your pores. If you tend to perspire, combine the water-based foundation with a dusting of face powder.

There is a great deal of controversy about whether or not large women should contour their faces. Some makeup artists think it can make the face look dirty. Coreen Cordova, a San Francisco makeup consultant, suggests you let a professional contour only half of your face. You should then look closely at your face. Properly applied contour is almost invisible. If you still feel the contouring makes a difference, do it. If not, don't waste your time.

Coreen, once a big woman said, "I can't stress enough how important makeup is for a big woman in making her feel good about herelf. It's not that the makeup does it, it's the self-esteem it represents."

Both Coreen and Jake agree that large women should not use contouring techniques to try to make their faces look thin. They both agree that kind of contouring makes the face look out of balance with the rest of a large woman's body. Jake feels contour should be used only to enhance the face. Blending is the key. If you can see the lines, you've failed. Use a sponge just like an eraser. Jake recommends using a dusty plum colored powder for contouring for all skin types. He says that will prevent the harsh lines shades of brown can cause.

Jake further advises, "Eyes frame the face in the same way that a picture is framed, so the eyelid should be neutral, perhaps a peach color. The outside of the eyelid should be accented with color. Be sure to leave a clear line between the eye and the blusher. Never use erase sticks made of wax and powder. The wax melts and causes creasing. If you do use a cover-up under your eyes, be gentle. The skin under the eyes is the thinnest on the face, and it can be easily stretched. Use three or four coats of mascara. Don't powder between coats, because that could make the mascara flake off. Don't shy away from glitter and glamour for evening. You should use natural-looking makeup during the day, but be adventurous in the evening. Strive for a complete look."

As Carole Shaw says, "Your smile is your best accessory, use it." If you don't think a smile makes a difference, walk into a room smiling and see how contagious it is. Take care of your smile. I know dentists are expensive, but your smile is priceless. Keep your teeth in good repair and, for heaven's sake, pay attention to your breath. There's no surer turn off than a well-groomed person with garlic breath.

How are you doing so far? Found anything that could use some work? Instead of another diet, put your energy and money where it's truly needed.

DIDN'T YOUR MOTHER EVER TELL YOU TO STAND UP STRAIGHT?

Posture is high on my list of priorities. I started worrying about my posture when my "Unknown Fat Person" photos revealed I was beginning to develop a "dowager hump" (protruding upper back). It's common in elderly women, and it seems to run in families. I'm hoping that by improving my posture now, I won't develop the hump. West Point study reports that about 90 percent of their new cadets don't know how to stand up straight. Despite our mother's nagging, no one has ever really taught us the fundamentals of good posture. A few exercises in gym class won't do the trick. The things I learned about posture in gym class hurt so much that I literally slumped over in defeat. Good posture doesn't mean you have to stand ramrod straight. Standing that straight puts a strain on joints and muscles.

Good posture means aligning the body so it can work more efficiently. Don't groan. As your body weight changes, you may need to realign your posture to compensate for your new weight distribution. This is true whether you gain or lose weight. Physiologists and specialists in biomechanics say ideal posture means your body weight is centered over the ankle bone and a vertical line would cut through the middle of the knee, hip, center of the shoulder tip, and the ear lobe. How do you stack

Proper Alignment for Good Posture

up? You'll probably notice it's almost impossible to judge by yourself. This is another exercise best accomplished with a partner.

You'll need a straight line for comparison—a piece of string with a light weight tacked to the ceiling works well. Stand next to the string so it falls parallel to the side of your body. Have your partner direct you so that the vertical line would cut through the appropriate points. It will probably hurt at first, because you will be trying too hard. Hold the good posture position with your eyes closed for a few seconds. Feel which muscles are pulling. How do your legs feel? What position are they in? Now relax for a moment and then, without coaching, try to resume this position. Have your partner correct your posture again. Feel it again. Relax again.

Again, try to resume the right position. This time concentrate on the one area that is most in need of correction. Maybe your chin sticks out too much. I developed that habit when I was a kid. I discovered that if you jut your chin out, it stretches the skin under the neck and your double chin will disappear. After years of trying to hide my chin, it became an unconscious habit. Whenever I think about my posture now, I automatically try to pull my chin in to its normal position. I've made a habit of reminding myself to practice good posture. It's best to work on one problem at a time. You may discover a problem you can't correct by yourself. That lower back pain could be caused by poor posture. Have it checked out.

Correct posture is not only good for you, it demonstrates self-confidence. Think about how you feel when you've just received a raise, or you're in love. Your body seems to puff up all by itself. Try to recapture that tall feeling as often as you can. Good posture is the best framework for clothes. Clothes will look better on a healthy, cared-for body, no matter what the size. A pair of well-poised shoulders makes any garment hang better.

If you seem tall, you'll carry your clothes better and you'll draw attention away from those areas of your body you don't want to emphasize. To seem taller than you are, use good posture. Look people in the eye or fix your gaze slightly above their eyes. This gives the impression that you're at least as tall, if not taller, than they are. Wear slightly higher heels, but avoid really high heels. They will only make a short person look out of balance. Avoid stiletto heels; they can also make you look unbalanced. Imagine you're a puppet whose whole weight is dangled from a string attached to the top of your head. Try it and feel how your neck straightens up. Feel how the space between your ribs expand. That's how tall feels.

YOUR VOICE SHOULD SOUND THE WAY YOU LOOK

Singers and radio announcers know it can take years to develop a well-modulated, unaffected voice. We may not have years to spend, but we can spare a few minutes with a tape recorder to find out how we can improve. If you have a high wispy voice or a Betty Boop giggle and you want to be taken more seriously, work on lowering your voice. Controlling your voice is a matter of using the right muscles and breathing correctly.

Record your voice when you're talking on the phone, then play it back several times. Is it harsh, shrill, too quiet, or too loud? Work on improving your problem area and repeat the exercise until you like what you hear. Some speech pathologists believe that pleasant, proper, clear speech is, the key to gaining acceptance for those considered outside normal standards. That's us, folks.

ARE YOU SPEAKING THE SAME LANGUAGE YOUR BODY IS?

Besides the mouth, hands and eyes are your most important instruments of communication. Pay attention to how you use your hands. Do they enhance what you have to say or are they distracting? Are you taking care of them? When was the last time you polished your nails? Did you know that touching your hair is considered a common gesture of flirtation? Maybe your mouth is saying no, but your body is saying yes.

I've heard several big people say everyone is always looking at them. If it's going to happen anyway, take advantage of the attention. Some people spend a fortune on getting other people to notice them. We have a built-in attention-getting device, and most of us don't use it. We're big. We're different. In this world of sameness, we have the advantage. Make good use of the attention. Make your body language work for you. Practice your body language by playing charades with a few friends. Instead of books and movies, act out different emotions. Think about how you use your body to convey each emotion. Practice in front of a mirror.

Practice walking gracefully and rhythmically. Practice sitting and standing gracefully. The way you hold your body tells the world how you're feeling. A video camera can help you study your body langauge. Seeing yourself on videotape will give you a really objective look at your body language. Try some role-playing situations such as a job interview. You may be amazed at the annoying gestures you have that you were never aware of.

HOW DO YOU SHAPE UP?

Fat and healthy are not contradictory terms. Are you taking care of your body? Remember, it's the only one you get. Are you getting plenty of sleep, eating good food, and getting exercise? Good health means good teeth, shiny hair, good complexion, and a pleasant personality. If you don't take care of the basics, then forget everything else. Lotions and potions won't compensate for bad health.

Ann Smith, author of *Stretch* and several other books on exercise, has come out with a small book of exercise for large people called *The Gifted Figure*. Ann wrote her book for "the person who is and probably always will be overweight according to the standard charts, but is not necessarily overweight in relation to individual build, body chemistry, and personality." Her system is based on safe, non-tiring stretching movements. Her exercises are easy to start no matter how long it's been since you last exercised.

Speaking of exercise, have you exercised your brain today? We make an impression with what we say as well as how we say it. I once had someone tell me I was so interesting to talk to that he forgot I was fat. Imagine the spell I cast. If you don't know the art of conversation, learn it. If you don't have a hobby, find one. Being able to talk intelligently with people could be one of the biggest weapons to overcome fatphobia.

Don't you feel better? Can you see that creating your image isn't a mysterious process? I bet you found out you are in pretty good shape image wise. If you think you don't have any areas to work on, you're not being honest. I still have areas I'd like to improve on. We all labor under misconceptions about our images. One of the most harmful misconceptions we have to overcome is the before and after myth. The before and after myth implies all fat people are bad and all thin people automatically become good. The truth is if you can't achieve the image you want when you're fat, you won't achieve it when you're thin. All the good things you hope for when you're thin are possible today.

There will be days when your new image doesn't seem to fit right. That's part of being human. I used to call the days that I felt out of sync my "fat days." I'd blame the scale. Now I give myself permission to have an off day. I don't like those kind of days, but I don't blame them on my fat. In fact, I had "fat days" even when I weighed 129 pounds. Don't be so hard on yourself. Sometimes I think we are our own worst critics. Lighten up a little!

YOU CAN HAVE MANY IMAGES

Another harmful misconception is that no image is better than a bad image. I used to think if I just blended in and tried to be inconspicuous, I'd be better off than if I tried to draw attention to myself. I now realize how destructive that attitude can be.

Fat Americans are making a terrible mistake when they don't project the kind of image they want. We've accepted fatphobia stereotypes by default. Our silence has been mistaken for consent. I didn't understand the importance of not having an image until I went shopping the other day. While I was in the checkout line, I noticed a big display of generic brand products. People were walking right by it. This prompted me to survey the shopping carts around me. Only one or two people had taken advantage of the considerable savings. Did the plain black and white boxes make that much of a difference? Do Jolly Green and Popin' Fresh make that much of an impression on us? If not having an image makes a difference in selling tissue, think of what that means for fat people. We can't afford to sit back and let people assume we don't care. Another destructive misconception is that each person is entitled to one image which must be maintained all the time. We must get this misconception from watching too many perfume commercials. I couldn't imagine any of the beautiful women in commercials sneaking off to the Mini-Mart for milk wearing pink curlers and no makeup. I assumed all those lovely ladies sprang from bed each morning protected by the magic spell of a fragrance I could never afford.

I was in for a shock when I had the opportunity to hire high fashion models. They came for their fittings looking more like they were going on a fishing trip than preparing for a glamorous fashion show. When the curtain rose, they were magnificent. And when I became a model, I understood why models don't waste their energy looking perfect all the time.

You don't have to look one way all the time to have a good image. Why waste your best look on the dishes? You don't have to make a career out of taking care of your image. As long as you know how to put it together at the right time, you'll be fine. There's also no right image for everyone. Hollywood and Madison Avenue have established a strict set of rules to define what is in fashion. If they keep us all heading in the same direction, we're all supposed to want the same merchandise. In the 1950s, this image obedience was at its peak. Some people still follow the lead of these fashion "authorities." Big Business is still trying to round off our corners so we'll be easier to fit.

THE DIFFERENCE BETWEEN STYLISH AND STYLE

To date, big women have been offered few fashion alternatives. Big women desperately need a sense of personal style. Wouldn't it be wonderful if all you big ladies with a hidden sense of style stepped forward so the rest of

Image

the world could learn to appreciate your uniqueness? Everyone has an image, but only a few people have personal style. Don't confuse personal style with stylishness. To be stylish, all you have to do is wear the latest fashions without regard for your personal needs. I think a lot of people who wear running clothes are doing it not because they run, but just to be stylish. To have personal style, you've got to have taste. You can't buy good taste, but you can learn how to develop it. More than the clothes themselves, personal style is the way you wear those clothes.

Being stylish can be boring. You can be fashionable and lack spirit. You can be perfectly groomed and still not be unique. When you have personal style, you trust your ability to select becoming, appropriate clothes that enhance your inner and outer selves. Being stylish means you conform to the prevailing fashion. It's a sign of insecurity and lack of imagination. Personal style means being true to yourself. When you find your personal style, you'll never have to compare or compete with anyone again. There's only *one* you.

When you find your personal style, you'll never have to worry about changes in style. The clothes may change, but you'll always know how to adapt them so they're contemporary and uniquely you. Developing a personal style means relearning the art of standing out. Standing out doesn't mean showing off. You don't have to stand out like a sore thumb.

One of fatphobia's big dangers is in forgetting our uniqueness. All we can see is the extra weight. That's why we have to learn to judge ourselves objectively. Don't be hard on yourself because you don't live up to some artificial standard of success. Find the real you. At the end of the chapter we'll do some exercises and experiments to help you regain your objectivity so you can recognize your personal style.

Is the exciting, interesting person inside you afraid to come out because of fatphobia? Are you rejecting an important part of your personality? Are you expressing all aspects of your personality? Are you realizing your potential?

I haven't always been tuned into my image. Not too long ago I was in an image prison. I felt compelled to project the only image I thought was appropriate for fat people. I'd try on nice clothes, but a little voice would say, "Fat people aren't supposed to wear sexy clothes or roller skate." Fatphobia stereotypes were denying some important aspects of my personality. I wouldn't buy the gym shorts and the shirt I needed for roller skating, so when it came time to go skating, I'd stay home because I didn't have anything to wear.

IMAGE GOALS

Do some serious thinking about all the roles you play. Who are you? I'm a writer/model/wife. My husband is an electrician/photographer/husband. My neighbor is a mother/bank teller. Make a list of all your roles. Try to be specific. You have to sort your roles out if you're going to find an image that is right for each of them.

Place your list in a conspicuous spot. I use my refrigerator door or bathroom mirror. Each time you notice the list think about what kind of image would be best for each role. Are there any roles you'd like to assume? Add them to the list. When you are satisfied that you've listed everything, you've defined your identity. You've discovered the varied elements that make your image unique. Now all you have to do is find a way to express them.

It's all a matter of personal style. Miss Piggy may think a pale blue silk blouse, pearl-gray pleated skirt, and a simple pillbox hat are the perfect attire for writing, but I like a ratty bathrobe or a pair of ragged jeans. Since I spend half of my time writing at home, half of my wardrobe is unfit for human viewing. My typewriter doesn't care how I look.

For business, I like well-tailored feminine suits that say I'm a professional. For those special intimate times with my husband, I like lacy lingerie. When I'm shopping or having lunch with friends, I prefer a classic, preppy look. Separate your roles to find your image goals.

Image goals help you get what you want. Image goals help define the problem so you can see the answer more clearly. From your list, select a role that's a problem for you. Think about which part of your personality you could improve to change the situation. Now think of how this change could be expressed in your image. Write it down. I know, it seems like a waste of time to write it down, but it helps you clarify your thinking.

Example:

Role: Secretary.

Problem: I want to become the boss's assistant.

Resource: I know I can do the job.

Solution: Show the boss I can do the job because I'm efficient.

Action: Project a more efficient image at work.

Role: _____

Problem: _____

Resource: _____

Solution: _____

Action: _____

Do this for all the roles where an image change might help solve a problem. These will be your image goals. When you've identified your image goals you'll know exactly where you are going with your image.

These exercises aren't meant to box you in. They are tools to help you focus your resources. We're such complex people that it's not always easy to see the improvements our image needs. We've made some progress toward defining the image we want. But have we missed anything? Isn't there more to image than body size and attitude? How can we express the relationship between your personality and the way you look?

In a 1940 textbook on dressing right, I found the perfect terms to express that relationship—*yin* and *yang*. Terms like masculine and feminine seemed so judgmental. *Yin* and *yang* are such beautifully simple words to describe opposites in nature. *Yin* means soft, gentle, quiet, small, light, and delicate. It doesn't imply a value judgment. *Yang* means big, bright, sleek, bold, and sophisticated. Since everyone is a different combination of both *yin* and *yang*, you can't really stereotype anyone. No one is either all Yin or all Yang. We should strive for a balance of *yin* and *yang* in ourselves, but one may dominate slightly. Are you Yin-dominated or a Yang-dominated? Find out by taking this test.

Yin people are often described as youthful, informal, active, outgoing, feminine. **Yin** clothing can be soft, feminine, lacy, flowing, fluffy, or frilly. It can also be casual, sporty, simple, practical, comfortable, informal, and unstructured.

Yang people are usually described as dynamic, powerful, reserved, dignified, dramatic, and assertive. **Yang** clothing is often described as tailored, sophisticated, elegant, dramatic, formal, structured, refined, and dignified.

Which best describes you? If you don't fit either category or you have equal elements of both, you are a combination, of **yin** and **yang** elements. After you have marked all four sections of the test, total the marks in each column. Each total indicates the rough percentage of your wardrobe or image that should be projected in each style.

Current Wardrobe

(Circle category that best describes you)

	Yin	Yang	Combination
1. Dresses			
2. Blouses			
3. Skirts			
4. Pants			
5. Coats			
6. Jackets/Sweaters			
7. Shoes/Purses			
8. Jewelry			
9. Hats			
10. Belts and Other Accessories			
Totals	%	%	%

Clothing Preference

(Circle category that best describes you)

	Yin	Yang	Combination
1. Dresses			
2. Blouses			
3. Skirts			
4. Pants			
5. Coats			
6. Jackets/Sweaters			
7. Shoes/Purses			
8. Jewelry			
9. Hats			
10. Belts and Other Accessories			
Totals	%	%	%

Big & Beautiful

Physical Image

(Circle category that best describes you)

		Yin	Yang	Combination
1.	Hair	Fair	Dark	_____
2.	Complexion	Fair	Dark	_____
3.	Height	5′4″ and under	5′6″ and over	5′5″
4.	Walking Style	Slow	Fast	_____
5.	Gestures	Open	Closed	_____
6.	Build	Small	Large	_____
7.	Expression	Outgoing	Reserved	_____
8.	Mannerisms	Natural	Dramatic	_____
9.	Movements	Slow	Fast	_____
10.	Coloring	Delicate	Vivid	_____
	Totals	%	%	%

Attitude and Lifestyle

(Circle category that best describes you)

		Yin	Yang	Combination
1.	Job	Low Pressure	High Pressure	_____
2.	Leisure	Relaxed	Active	_____
3.	Temperament	Positive	Negative	_____
4.	Ambition	Low	High	_____
5.	Stress Level	Low	High	_____
6.	Attitude	Submissive	Dominant	_____
7.	Attitude	Intuitive	Analytical	_____
8.	Attitude	Idealistic	Realistic	_____
9.	Attitude	Youthful	Mature	_____
10.	Attitude	Natural	Sophisticated	_____
	Totals	%	%	%

Image

How did you do? Did you notice any inconsistencies? Do you have a *yin* clothing preference and a closet full of *yang* clothes? Is your personality *yang*-dominated and your physical image *yin*? We'll work on problems like these in the next few chapters. I hope finding image development is an exciting experience. It's certainly a lot more fun than dieting, and the results will last a lot longer than the weight loss. Dieting is reduction, image development is growth. You've already learned to be more objective in thinking about your attitude, identity, and personality.

As a final exercise in this part of your image growth, plan a spa weekend or slumber party with a male or female friend. Pratice some of the suggested exercises in this chapter. Image development doesn't have to be a painful process. Have fun with it.

This is a summary of what you might want to do to improve your image!

- Try a new hairstyle
- Get a professional manicure and/or pedicure
- New eyeglasses or contact lenses
- Take a class such as dancing, singing, public speaking, or modeling
- Have a makeover
- Read a self-improvement book

Photo courtesy of YOUNG STUFF a division of Stout Sportswear Group.

Chapter 5

THE LANGUAGE OF DESIGN

- I have a hard time making up my mind when I shop.
- I never look as together as other women do.
- I hate my clothes.
- Sometimes I feel like I'm hiding behind my clothes.
- I'm stuck with the same look I had years ago.

If you agreed with one or more of these statements, you're normal. All women hesitate when considering these statements, even the experts. Just because our bodies are bigger, doesn't mean we're any different. I've talked with women of all sizes and shapes, and everyone has the same complaints. We want clothes that enhance our appearance. We have a clothing crisis. We think everyone except us has an easy time finding clothes.

Since I've never been smaller than a size 14, for more than a few weeks in my life, I assumed all the attractive clothes were a size 10 or smaller. I asked a friend if she found it easier to buy clothes now that she's reduced from a size 16 to a size 7. She said, "It's a pain to be a size 7. It seems like everyone is a size 7." By the time she has the money and the urge to shop, everything nice is gone.

FINDING GOOD-LOOKING CLOTHES IN LARGE SIZES: A PROBLEM

There are certain problems that are unique to big women, but finding nice clothes isn't necessarily one of them. We're not alone in our frustration with the fashion industry. We do have some special problems in finding certain kinds of clothes. Georgia, Jane, and Barbara express complaints voiced by 90 percent of the women I interviewed.

Georgia: "I refuse to put myself in the category of being too obese to wear the "in" styles. I'll do without before I'll wear polyester pants with elastic waists, or tunic tops. I won't make myself look matronly. I'm only thirty years old. I don't and won't look thirty years old. I have one friend in particular who could look younger and nicer, but she sticks with polyester pants and big tops."

Barbara: "Too many of the stores assume that someone who's fat doesn't care what they look like. Just give them pants and an overblouse that look like they were handed down from young grandmother. When I got to the point where I had to go to some of those large size shops, I went through the phone book and found there were very few. I had terrible experiences. These stores only had around the house sportswear. I need something to wear to work. Big stores like Macy's aren't bad, but we don't have the choices 'normal' people have available to them. My biggest gripe is the choice is polyester or polyester."

Jane: "I'd like to see clothes made a little bit sexier. If you're large you probably have a good bust, which may be your only good feature. I resent buying things with high necklines. I have a good tan and I'd like to show it.

I also resent manufacturers who say, 'Oh, we've got a large market of fat women, so let's jack the prices up.' They know now we want to look nice, so they make us pay more. They say it's because large size clothes require

Design

more material. Keep sending in the 'I'm Mad as Hell' coupons from *Big, Beautiful Woman* magazine and maybe they'll get the message."

What are the designers, manufacturers, and buyers thinking about? Instead of trying to talk us into buying what they're trying to sell, why aren't they listening more carefully to our needs? Where did they get the idea that all petite women want young, cutesy clothes? Or that all big women want matronly polyester dresses? Or that all pregnant women want conservative necklines? Or that all tall women want tailored clothes?

And while we're at it, what about the crazy sizing system? I'm too big for most 18/20s, but I'm too small for 38s. Most large size stores start at size 38. A size 18½ dress fits beautifully, but sportswear doesn't usually come in half sizes. Instead of worrying about starving myself into a size 12, I now have to worry about finding any size to fit me.

A few other women have complaints about size and fit. How many times have you thought the same things?

Pam: "I don't know why this is, but in most stores you find a nice selection of 12s and 14s, but by the time you get to the 16s, there are only three rags hanging there. Either they don't buy any or they buy a lot and they sell out. Doesn't anybody realize that there is a market there? When you are a 14, there are fashionable outfits. But suddenly, in size 16, they assume you don't want to be fashionable anymore."

Bev: "That's a problem. There's no place in between. Some shops go to a 16. If they do have things in larger sizes, they think everyone who's heavy has arms the size of a tree. The clothes aren't well-proportioned. If they fit in the waist, there's room for another person in the bottom. If they fit at the bottom, you can't get the top zipped. Then you get the ones that fit in the waist and the crotch is down to your knees."

Kathy: "I dislike the way they make some of the pants. They don't fit. Have you ever tried on pants only to find legs are huge? I'm walking around in Clem Kadiddlehopper pants. Three of my thighs could fit into one leg of those pants. They're not attractive. When you start getting into a size 32 or 34 pants you have to try on a lot of different pants to find one pair that fits."

It feels great to let off some steam. I get tired of being damned if I do and damned if I don't. Why can't we have as many different departments as the "normal" size women? Large women make up over a third of the female population. Go into any department store and you'll find juniors, junior miss, misses, miss petite, junior teen, sportswear, career wear—all in sizes up to 18. Where do they put our clothes? They're all jammed together in one small department hidden in the darkest corner of the basement.

Can't they see there are young big women, short big women, and tall big women? How about a career department for big women? They could call it "Becoming a Great Big Success." Why not? What's the problem?

I'm repeating myself so I'll be sure the message sinks in completely. We've heard the old stories so many times that it may take a little repetition for them to really have any impact. It's okay to be different. It's nice to be unique. We don't have to look like everyone else to be accepted. Isn't it just common sense to try to look the best you can, rather than trying to look like someone else? The best thing about the large size fashion shows I've seen or worked in is that the models represent a wide cross section of the population than the models in regular fashion shows. I've worked with tall, short, young, old, barely big, and very large models. The variety makes the show more interesting. I hope we can keep the pressure on so that it stays that way.

Most regular fashion designers and manufacturers have such narrow standards that only perfect size 8s need apply. Most designers find one special model whose looks and measurements fit their ideal. They design a complete line of clothes for this ideal model. I don't want to see size 18 become that kind of a standard for the large size industry. If we can build a space shuttle, you'd think we could design clothes with more than one kind of person in mind.

It's not as though we don't have the money. My surveys indicate large size women would spend twice what we do now if the clothes we liked were available. Kay, a big, tall housewife from San Francisco, told a group she had to buy a new dress for a wedding. She said, "I was ready to buy. I needed something. I had a checkbook, credit cards, or cash. But did I find anything? I never find anything! I went home and made an outfit out of some fabric I had stuck away in a closet. I couldn't find a camisole, so I had to use my pajama top." Most big women say they have similar problems. If they can't find it in the stores and they can't make it, they go without.

The manufacturers say they're interested. At least they talk a lot about our problem. Last season I went to a large size fashion show held by one of the major department store chains. After the show, a half dozen manufacturers' representatives asked the audience what we really wanted. There was a lot of talk, but, as far as I can tell, no action.

I asked several people in the industry why large size women aren't getting what we ask for. Everyone points the fingers at everyone else. When I talked to the owner of a small specialty store, he said the problem exists because the major chain store buyers aren't ordering the innovative merchandise from the small manufacturers. The major chain store buyer said it's the fault of manufacturers who don't make the styles available. The manufacturers said it's the chain store's fault for not buying the new styles. Meanwhile, we have no decent clothes to wear.

It's up to us to straighten out this mess. Designers, manufacturers and buyers are so busy watching each other and trying to figure out what to do next, they've forgotten about their customers. The audience at the fashion show had the opportunity to talk to the manufacturers, but they couldn't communicate their ideas in terms the manufacturers understood.

We can solve that problem by learning to speak the language of the fashion industry. In this chapter we'll learn how to use this new language to tell the industry what we want. We will learn how to recognize and understand the principles and elements, so we can overcome the fatphobia stereotypes. We'll also learn how to express our personality, identity, and attitude in clothes and accessories we select.

I hope you're not disappointed because this isn't the typical "Ten Easy Steps to Putting Your Makeup on Better" kind of book. You can find plenty of that kind of advice in any magazine rack. Makeup, accessories, hairstyle, and clothing details are the kind of image elements that must be fresh and up-to-date. They shouldn't be static because their job is to provide newness and variety.

THE PRINCIPLES OF GOOD DESIGN

The advice you'll find in magazines and at makeup counters works for us, too. We've got all the basic equipment, maybe a little more of some, but the advice still applies. Instead, we need to look at the basics. We need to rediscover the principles of good design lost in the fashion rush to sameness. One quick glance at any high fashion magazine will tell you most designers have strayed too far from the truth of the human body. I'm all for fashion giving us something new to look at, but not at the expense of good design.

I've always thought I could design better clothes for big women than the people who make a fortune designing today's clothes. You've probably thought the same thing. With a little training and some money, I'm sure we could succeed. I once heard a designer tell a crowd of would-be designers that she couldn't sketch a straight line or sew a stitch. She said, "You don't need those talents to succeed in fashion. You need guts and the ability to promote." With an attitude like that, no wonder so many clothes are ugly and impractical.

Good design is based on rules that have applied for centuries. A good designer doesn't have to plaster his or her signature all over their clothes. Good design is its own signature. Even the inexperienced eye can see the mark of a professional. The principles of design are *balance, scale, proportion, rhythm,* and *emphasis.* The elements are *line, shape, contrast, texture,* and *color.* Texture and color will be discussed in Chapter 7.

Good design is an organized plan or a solution to a problem. Good clothing design is both. In clothing design, structure refers to the outline or silhouette of the clothes. Structure also includes the way a garment is put together (i.e., the many panels of a gore skirt). Details, such as lace and trim, are often referred to as applied design, since they are added after a garment is almost finished. When we judge the design of a garment we'll want to look at the structural and applied design.

Balance: Focus an Asset

We will be concerned with *balance*. Because we have such a small space to work with, proper balance is essential. Balance implies choice, and you need to make a choice about each part of your body. Are you going to enhance it, disguise it, or ignore it? Perhaps you look in the mirror and all you can see are your hips. In your mind, they're out of proportion compared to the rest of your body. Most fashion experts would tell you to disguise your flaws. But that means you would emphasize the negative. Concentrating on your body flaws is like being on a diet. If you are constantly worrying about staying away from food, you'll always be thinking about food. I would rather concentrate on the positive. We all have them.

I've known women who work so hard at trying to hide a problem they end up spotlighting it. One big, middle-aged woman wears caftans all the time because she thinks they hide her big hips. The caftan also hides a lot of her good features. It's ironic that her caftans are so shapeless that the only part of her body you see when she walks is her hips. She has totally defeated her purpose by trying too hard. There are better ways to solve her problem.

From now on, our philosophy should be: if you don't want people to look at something, what *do* you want them to look at? If you want them to notice something, how are you going to direct their attention to that spot? This means you have to stop believing the goal is to dress thin. If you are more than ten pounds over what you think you should be, dressing thin doesn't work. Ten pounds is about all you can cover up with clothing styles and color. Instead of thinking thin, think balanced. Balance gives you more options. Thin implies there is only one acceptable body type. Every body type can achieve a pleasing balance.

According to the traditional approach, all you could do to disguise big hips was to wear a dark, A-line skirt, and pray that doing one hundred leg lifts daily would help. Instead of hiding your hips, focus on an asset. If you have a nice neck and bustline, why not direct attention there? A light-colored top with an open neckline would balance a hip problem nicely. A small amount of padding in the shoulders or horizontal stripes can balance big hips.

Because of years of conditioning, new ideas can be hard to get used to. So it's a good idea to start slowly. Build your confidence gradually. Try small changes at first. Drastic changes could be hazardous to your ego.

Balance is achieved both formally and informally. Formal balance means both sides look equal. A double-breasted blazer is an example of formal balance. This kind of balance can be safe, but boring if it's overdone. Informal balance means unequal parts are arranged to create balance. Think of two kids on a seesaw, if the kids are the same weight you have a formal balance. If one is heavier than the other, you have to adjust their positions to achieve balance. A one-shouldered evening dress is an example of informal balance. Another example is a small, bright scarf balancing an otherwise dull dress. Artists and interior designers use the same principles in their work.

Balance can also be thought of as harmony between the elements that create the image. You achieve harmony when every part works together as a pleasing whole. For example, shorter skirts tend to look better with low heels. Longer skirts look better with higher heels. You have to avoid inconsistencies to achieve total harmony. Don't be afraid to experiment. Just be sure you have a full length mirror to check the results. Total harmony can also be boring if overdone. (A big hat on a small person will look out of balance.)

Line

Without *line* you couldn't have design. Lines form the boundaries and connect the parts of a design. Many people think line is the most important element of design. You can create a specific mood by the way you use line in a design. The direction of a line can create a sense of movement and symbolic meaning. And, of course, you can create optical illusions with line.

The lines of a garment divide the space of your body into smaller areas of interest. For example, the line created by a contrasting yoke would divide a dress into two spaces, one large and one small. The using of line in certain ways can evoke predictable emotional responses. Cover the answers and guess what emotions these lines are supposed to suggest.

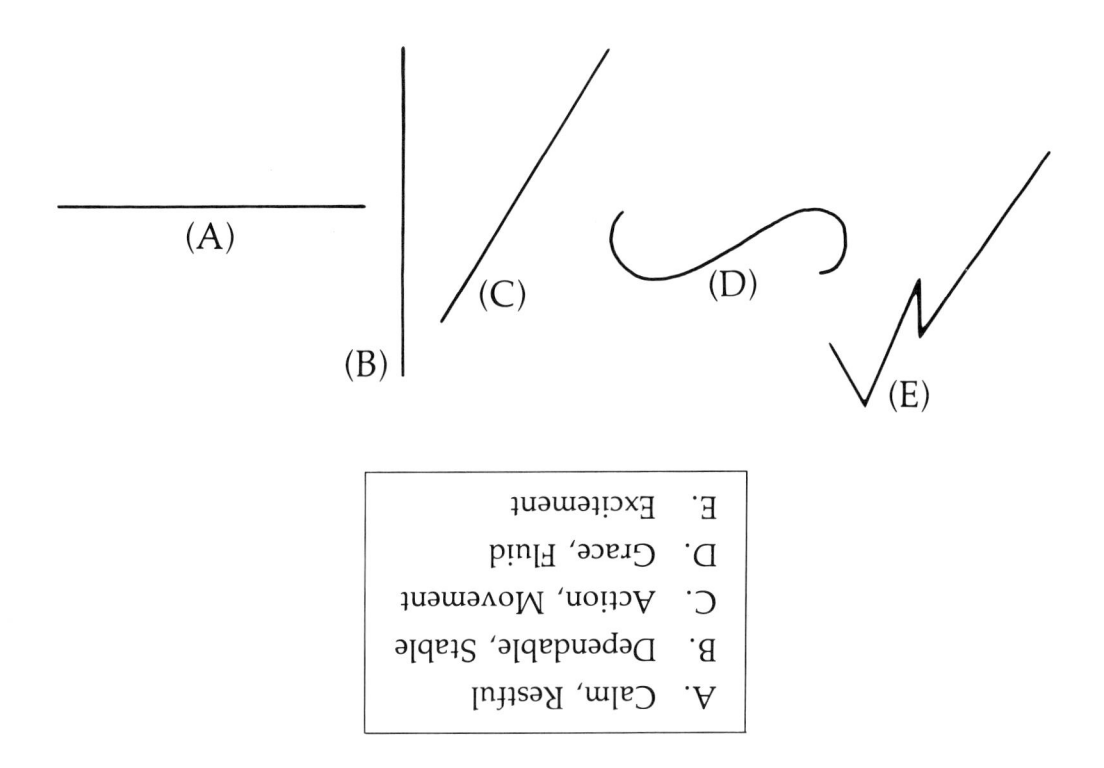

(A)

(B)

(C)

(D)

(E)

A. Calm, Restful
B. Dependable, Stable
C. Action, Movement
D. Grace, Fluid
E. Excitement

How can you use line in your image? Think about a hairstyle. The way your hair is arranged creates lines. A curly, unstructured look will make a person look more Yin, and would also help to balance too-wide shoulders. A straight, tailored cut would create a Yang feeling, and would focus attention on the facial features.

Big & Beautiful

83

A skirt hem that falls at the fullest part of the calf will make the leg look shorter and heavier.

A skirt hem that falls at a narrow part of the leg such as just below the knee tends to make the leg look longer and more shapely.

Proportion and Scale

Proportion and *scale* go together. These are two of the most important design elements for us to consider. For a large woman, proportion can make or break her outfit. Unfortunately, most of us don't even know what proportion means or how to use it to our advantage. Proportion is the relationship of one part to the other parts. The basic laws of proper proportion were developed by the ancient Egyptians. Proper proportion can vary with each body. Hemlines are an area where proportion is important. The best proportion is usually achieved when the hemline falls at the smallest part of the leg. This is usually the ankle, below the knee, or slightly above the knee. When the hemline falls in the fullest part of the leg, such as mid-calf or thigh, it makes the leg look shorter and heavier. This information can help legs that are too skinny or too heavy.

Design

Scale refers to the part of a design being balanced. If you are a big, big woman, you should wear large prints and accessories. Tiny prints and small jewelry look out of scale on a big woman. The same principle applies to sleeves and collars. Any oversized or undersized detail can look funny. Our grand scale must be taken into consideration, but it doesn't have to be minimized.

Rhythm

Rhythm refers to the pleasing sense of motion you achieve with continuity of design. When the eye makes a smooth transition from one area of a design to another you've achieved a good rhythm. We can use rhythm to direct attention to our assets. If you don't consider rhythm in selecting fashion, you can end up sending a confusing image message. Let's say we met Helen on the street. She's wearing a large hat with a red flower, a bright print dress, ornate Indian turquoise jewelry, textured hose, fancy sandals, and carrying a green alligator purse. You probably wouldn't know what to look at first. So we give Helen a lesson in rhythm. The next time you see her, she has on a plain dress with one striking squash blossom necklace, and a pair of beautiful matching earrings.

Now our friend has control of her image. She is using her wonderful taste in jewelry and rhythm to focus our attention on her personality area. With the confusion of Helen's first outfit, we missed the fact that she has wonderful blue eyes, the color of the jewelry she loves. Now the first thing we notice is the interesting necklace, which we follow up to the earrings and that leads us right to her expressive blue eyes.

The key to the successful use of rhythm is subtlety. Don't be obvious. Watch out for decorative designs that might clash with the structure of your outfit. Be aware of the textures, shapes, and contrasts you put together. People see you as a whole, so all parts of your image need to harmonize with each other. Rhythm is the way you tie together the areas you want to emphasize.

Emphasis

Emphasis is the dessert of image-making. Emphasis highlight is the aspect of your personality most important in that situation. Careful use of emphasis is the best tool you have to express your individuality. What you emphasize will change according to your goal. Emphasis should enhance your image, but not dominate it. Sometimes it's hard to decide what to emphasize. You can emphasize color, texture, structural details, applied designs, physical characteristics, or personality traits. You may be tempted to emphasize all of them. Don't. You'll lose the impact. The purpose is to draw attention to something interesting. When you emphasize everything, you emphasize nothing. Every time you look in the mirror, you should see one dominant area. It should be the area that will get your message across most effectively. You'll also want to emphasize one or two subordinate areas to balance the effect. Needless to say, all areas of emphasis should be positive.

Keep in mind that the area you choose and the way you emphasize it will create a mood. Let's say you have long, silky, jet-black hair. You want to get the attention of a certain accountant who works in your building. Long, freshly washed hair with an attractive ornament might be all he needs to speak up. One final word of caution. Emphasis is powerful magic, so don't get carried away. Don't overemphasize a good feature if it will expose a poor one. Bright red lipstick may be the perfect thing to emphasize a cupid bow mouth, but if you have rotten front teeth it may not be your best choice.

There are two rules to remember in working with emphasis. When you repeat a line, color, shape etc., you emphasize that element of your image. Strong contrasts work the same way. If you have a round face and you select round frames for your glasses, you will be emphasizing the roundness of your face. If you have red hair and you wear a green sweater, you will be emphasizing your hair color by using strong contrast. Overemphasizing isn't a good idea. Let's update the old point system to keep us from overemphasizing and spoiling our new image.

Design

THE LESS IS BEST GUIDE TO EMPHASIS

- Score five points for every dominant area of emphasis.

- Score two points for each subordinate area of emphasis.

- Score one point for each incidental thing area of emphasis.

Your total score could be between ten and fifteen points.

We'll use our friend who likes Indian jewelry as an example. In Helen's first outfit, the large, hat, bright dress, and turquoise jewelry would each count five points. That's fifteen points already. I'd add two points each for the red flower, textured hose, fancy sandals, and the expensive green alligator purse. That brings Helen's total to twenty-three points. Since she emphasized everything, we didn't notice anything in particular.

Now lets check her new image. Her attractive necklace is her dominant area. That counts for five points. The earrings and eyes are two points each, making nine points. Someone might notice her smile, unusual ring, and attractive sandals. Add three more points, which gives a total of twelve. Her new image doesn't suffer from overemphasis.

We've covered a lot of material so here is a quick review to help you remember the important elements and principles. The next chapter will show you how to apply these new tools to help you become a big, beautiful person.

REVIEW

Balance: Achieve balance in proportion, color, texture, emphasis, scale, and rhythm.

Scale: This means the size of parts in relationship to the whole picture. The right scale depends on the size of the person.

Proportion: Achieve a pleasing relationship between the parts of a design. Critical for big women.

Rhythm: How the eye moves from one area of your image to another. If the eye moves smoothly and pauses in the right places, you've done a good job.

Emphasis: Where the eye stops. This should be planned with care.

Line: Forms the boundaries and decorations of a design. It can be used to create a mood, focus attention, and carry out a theme.

Big &
Beautiful

Photo courtesy of Lane Bryant.

Chapter 6

BALANCE AND EMPHASIS: THE NEW RULES

Dress for Failure Fatphobia Rules

1. Don't wear pretty colors or stripes. Someone might notice you're fat. (As if they are going to miss all 200 plus pounds, right?)

2. Do wear drab colors. They will make you look so slim, no one will notice you at all.

3. Don't wear belts. Only people who weigh less than 140 pounds are allowed to have waistlines.

4. Never wear makeup, hairstyles, or accessories to enhance your image—people might notice you have a personality.

5. Don't embarrass people by wearing sexy, provocative clothing. Everyone knows fat people don't have sex lives. That's why only one or two companies make wedding dresses and maternity clothes for big women.

It seems like we're the first generation to grow up without a strict set of fashion rules. I vaguely remember all the "dos and don'ts" of the fifties and early sixties: don't wear gold shoes in the daytime unless you're a hooker; don't carry a black purse with brown shoes unless you're color blind. At least then I felt I knew where I stood.

Lately, it seems that each season we have a new set of fashion rules to follow. Most of the time, the rules seem to depend on what the stores are trying to sell. If they have copper shoes to sell, the experts swear it's chic to wear metallic shoes in the daytime. With so many new rules each season, we don't have any rules we can trust.

The only rules that have survived the last few decades are the rules that tell fat people how to dress. And we're still living by those rules. They were designed to diminish our presence. No wonder we have a hard time being taken seriously. The **Dress for Failure** rules have made us almost invisible. Add to the list of fatphobia **Dress for Failure** rules by thinking about the rules you automatically rely on when you shop. You have to identify the rules before you can begin to change them.

The fatphobia **Dress for Failure** rules are based on prejudices and misconceptions. At one time, the fatphobia rules helped people achieve a goal: to make us invisible. But, like most rules, they have outlived their usefulness. Though we no longer need or want to be invisible, we're still dressing by those outdated rules. We need a new set of rules that will help us redefine our image. We need guidelines we can trust, but they have to be flexible enough to allow for individual differences. We must learn to balance our image with the principles and elements of design.

These principles and elements of design were introduced in the last chapter. These concepts help demystify fashion. We can use that information to improve our image. We want to create designs that will flatter our shapes. We want to learn how to combine the elements and principles to create comfortable, becoming, and appropriate clothes that send out the right image message.

Good design expresses your individuality, suits your lifestyle, and enhances your physical image. Creating good design isn't nearly as hard as it may seem. The principles and elements of design are tools we can use to achieve a new image.

We'll examine each area of your body, showing you how you can use either emphasis or balance to achieve a better image. The object is not to make you look thinner, it's to make you look well-proportioned. You have to decide whether to emphasize or balance an area. Forget the **Dress for Failure**. We're going to rewrite the rule book.

You can select an area you would like to emphasize and find a different way to apply the guideline each day next week. For example, you might want to emphasize your shapely legs: Monday you could try wearing colored or textured hose; Tuesday you might wear a skirt with a slit; and Wednesday you could wear a skirt with a ruffled hem. You could select a different area each day: Monday you might work on drawing attention to your face; Tuesday your hands; and Wednesday your legs. Before you buy anything new, apply these guidelines to what you have in your closet. See if anyone notices the area you're emphasizing. If no one notices, try something new the next day. Analyze each success, and try to duplicate it with each new area of emphasis. Images are built by working on them everyday.

You can use this information to balance an area you feel uncomfortable with. Try to discover a new way to balance the problem area every day.

If you feel your calves are a bit large, you might try straight leg pants on Monday, raising your skirt hem to a smaller part of your leg on Tuesday, and could experiment with darker hose on Wednesday.

After you've practiced balancing and emphasizing, try combining both techniques in the same look. For example, when you shop for a new dress, you might look for a style that would enhance your well-developed bustline and balance your short legs. Some of the ideas may seem strange at first, but give yourself time to get used to them. It may take a few days of experimenting before someone comments on your new appearance. It doesn't necessarily mean they haven't noticed. If you allow yourself to be more attractive, someone will notice.

Now I will discuss how to use emphasis and balance to deal with problems you may have in one of the six areas of your body: head; neck and shoulders; bust, upper arm, torso, and waist; hips and fanny; legs and feet; and height.

HEAD

Emphasis: Your head, face, and hair are your major personality areas. The head is, therefore, the most important area to emphasize. Hats draw attention to the face and head, but be sure you're a hat person before you try this technique. It takes a special kind of authority to wear a hat well. The color of your makeup and accessories can draw attention to your head. So can an interesting neckline. A good haircut is another good way to emphasize your head.

Balance: The head can sometimes appear too small or too large for your body. A full hairstyle or a hat can help balance a too-small head. Sleek, close-cropped hairstyles give the illusion of a smaller head. Making the shoulders seem wider (for a too-small head) or narrower (for a too-large head) also help to balance an out-of-proportion head.

NECK AND SHOULDERS

Emphasis: Open necklines, interesting necklaces, off-the-shoulder or single shoulder designs, upswept hair, interesting colors and collars help to draw attention to the neck and shoulder area. If you want to show off your lovely neck and soft shoulders, expose or decorate them.

Balance: If you have a short neck, avoid clutter at the neckline. Open necklines and scoop necklines can help balance a short neck. Focusing attention higher (face and hair), or lower (bustline) also works. Avoid high collars—if you have a long neck, break the long line or fill up the area. Cowl-neck and turtleneck designs tend to make your neck seem shorter.

Scarves, ascots, chokers, multiple necklaces, and multiple layers of clothing, such as a sweater over a blouse, will help to fill in a long neck. Sometimes the best solution is to move the center of emphasis away from the neck.

To offset wide shoulders you can make the lower part of your body appear wider with soft, full skirts. This will give the illusion of better proportion. Avoid padded shoulders, puff and cap sleeves, and wide necklines. Sleeves that don't define the shoulder seam can also help to balance wide shoulders. Narrow shoulders, especially if combined with large hips or thighs, can make you look like a pear. Padded shoulders can make you look better proportioned. Raglan sleeves, dolman sleeves, drop shoulders, and regular set-in sleeves all look better with a little padding. Good fit is essential, otherwise you look sloppy. A top that is too loose or too tight will emphasize small shoulders. Soft fullness at the shoulders can make them seem larger. Light colors, bright prints, and horizontal stripes are good ways to create the illusion of balance. Sloping shoulders can give the body a dejected, droopy look, so work on your posture. Since the problems of narrow and sloping shoulders are similar, invest in some pin-in shoulder pads. Set-in sleeves create a square shoulder look, and choosing the right kind of sleeve can alleviate this problem. Experiment with different types of full sleeves to see which works best to balance your sloping shoulders.

BUST, UPPER ARM, TORSO, AND WAIST

Emphasis: Baring your bust, upper arms, torso, and waist with halter tops, open midriffs, plunging necklines, and tight clothing will definitely emphasize it. Tops with light colors and bright prints will draw attention to the upper body. Belts, long necklaces, and scarves also focus attention on your upper body especially if they contrast strongly in color. Ruffles, bows, breast pockets, tube tops, and puffy sleeves will emphasize the breast and upper arms. Wide sleeves and varying sleeve lengths call attention to the waist and upper body.

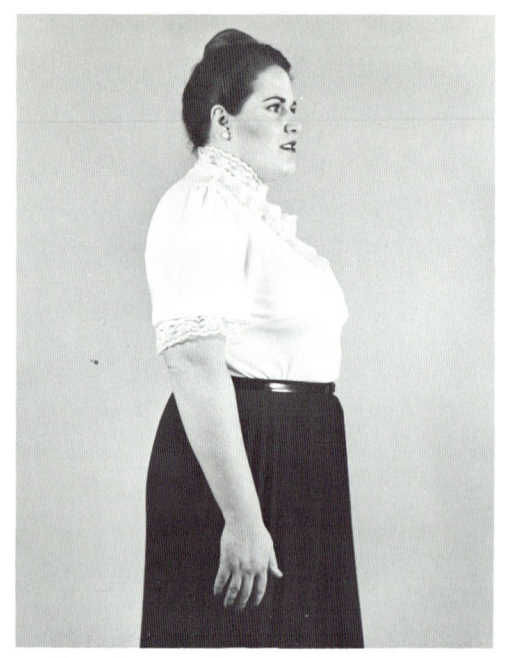

A short sleeve tends to emphasize the bustline and cut short any streamlined effect you may wish to create.

A longer sleeve draws the eye away from the bust area to areas you may wish to emphasize such as your hands or hairstyle.

Balance: The problems of balancing too-large or too-small busts are often similar. Soft gathers and controlled fullness help camouflage both. Pay particular attention to the hip and leg area when you are trying to balance a bust problem. A small bust can look smaller if it is compared to a very full skirt. Once again, the best solution often is to move the center of attention either higher or lower than the bust. Slightly flared garments will move the eye away from the bust. Bright colors and prints can sometimes fill out a small bust. Avoid high wasitlines, which draw attention to the bust.

Many of us have full upper arms. Sleeveless or short, tight sleeves often make the problem worse, but this doesn't mean we're forever doomed to wear long sleeves. Full, short sleeves, such as butterfly or puffed sleeves, can camouflage larger upper arms. Sleeves that stop at or below the elbow work well. Long, straight sleeves or long, full sleeves help to balance full upper arms. Rather than trying to hide the problem, why not move attention away from that area to the legs, feet, hands, or face?

Wearing a slightly longer skirt can help to balance a long torso, but pay attention to proportion. A too-long skirt can make you look dowdy. High or drop waistlines help a long torso because they move the eye away from the problem. To divide a look at your natural waistline, select a belt the same color as your pants, shorts, or skirt to offset the long torso line. If you are shortwaisted, move the waistline up under the bust or down to the hip. This gives the illusion of better balance. Flared, waistless styles are another solution. A belt the same color as your blouse will make your torso seem longer. Hiphugger pants will make your torso look longer. If you're tall enough, long tunics and overblouses will work, if they don't look sloppy.

If you have a large waist, the most obvious solution is to draw attention away from it. Emphasizing your shoulders or enhancing your hands and feet are good alternatives. Vests, tunics, and semi-fitted tops are good, but make sure they're properly proportioned. You don't have to avoid belts if you're large-waisted. A belt the same color as your clothes can define the waist and actually make it look smaller, if the overall look is well-proportioned. Belts at hip level are another solution. Semi-fitted jackets can suggest a waist without making you seem bulkier. If your waist is small, elastic waistbands add thickness to the waist. Gathers or pleats around the waist will make it seem bigger. Brightly colored belts also make the waist look larger. Full, unbelted dresses and tunics focus attention at the yoke or hem, and, if they are the right length can be another good solution.

HIPS AND FANNY

Emphasis: There are times when you may want to emphasize the lower half of your body. You might want to balance a top-heavy look, or your boyfriend or husband just might like looking at your fanny. Plaids, wide horizontal stripes, bright colors, pleats, gathers, tight clothes, clingy or heavy fabric, and hiphugger pants will emphasize this area.

Balance: Dark colors and flared skirts will help balance large hips and fanny. Light color tops and interesting necklines are another solution. Colors, jewelry, and scarves are great ways to direct attention away from the hips. Padded shoulders, especially if you have narrow or sloping shoulders, will do a lot to balance your look. Skirts and slacks that are slightly loose are better than tight clothes. If you want to wear a pleated skirt, select a sunburst rather than a box pleats. Stitched pleats can work, but they have to be stitched down to the right point below your waist to be flattering. Small hips can make you look top-heavy, even if you don't have a full bust. Light colored fabrics, interesting prints, gathers, and pleats can help fill out the hip area. Pay particular attention to your upper body in trying to balance too-small hips. Be aware that too much emphasis of bustline and shoulders can make your hips look even smaller.

LEGS AND FEET

Emphasis: Skirts with sexy slits, textured hose, interesting shoes, short hemlines, polish on your toenails, interesting socks, and boots are all ways to emphasize your feet and legs.

Balance: Pants, long skirts, simple shoes, and neutral hose are obvious ways to balance heavy or thin legs. These solutions are valid, but they're not very creative. In the previous chapter, we discussed how the length of your skirt can create the illusion of a smaller or larger legs. Dark hose will make heavy legs look smaller. Keeping the skirt, stockings, and shoes the same color also draws attention away from heavy legs. Light-colored hose add the illusion of weight to thin legs. Drawing attention to the area above the waist is another way to deal with problems in the leg and foot area.

HEIGHT

Emphasis: To emphasize your height or appear taller, use unbroken vertical lines and one-color outfits. Slim fitting slacks, long slim sleeves, fitted jackets, silky fabrics that move with the body, simple belts, and shoulder to hemline seaming all elongate your body. Shorter jackets can sometimes

Balance & Emphasis

Photo courtesy of Lane Bryant.

make you look taller by exposing more of your legs. Raised or empire waistlines have the same effect.

If you want to appear shorter, wear garments with strong contrast on the top and bottom. Wide belts, horizontal lines, full skirts, plaids, large prints, loose clothing, bulky fabrics, a wide variety of colors, and lots of lace and frills will all make you seem shorter. Skirts that are full or short are the most effective ways to shorten the body, so you have to watch your proportions carefully.

Everyone's body is unique. You may sometimes find yourself having to emphasize and balance the same area. That's why the simple "dos and don'ts" of the past don't really work. Achieving the right balance isn't always easy. At least you have more of a choice now. Work at balancing or emphasizing one problem area at a time. Don't try to create a whole new wardrobe in one day. Don't dismiss a possible solution just because it seems to violate the old fatphobia rules. Be flexible enough to find the right solution for you. Try to think of other ways to apply the elements and principles of design to solve your particular problems. The guidelines I've proposed aren't the only answers. Their main purpose is to get you to think about your body and your image in a different way. There is never just one solution.

I wanted to talk a little more about proportion in relation to balance and emphasis. Proper proportion is different for everyone. To discover what proportions are right for you, measure yourself (in inches) from head to toe. Now, measure your head, and divide the length of your body by the length of your head. The average person is seven to seven and one-half heads tall. Fashion illustrators draw models that are eight to eight and one-half heads tall. That's why when you order something from a catalog it sometimes won't look the same on you as it did in the picture.

Now divide your height in half, and find the halfway point on your body. This is your personal danger zone. Never divide your outfit at this point—don't wear jackets or drop-waist designs that stop at this point. De-emphasize this area. Dividing yourself at the halfway point will make you

Body Proportion

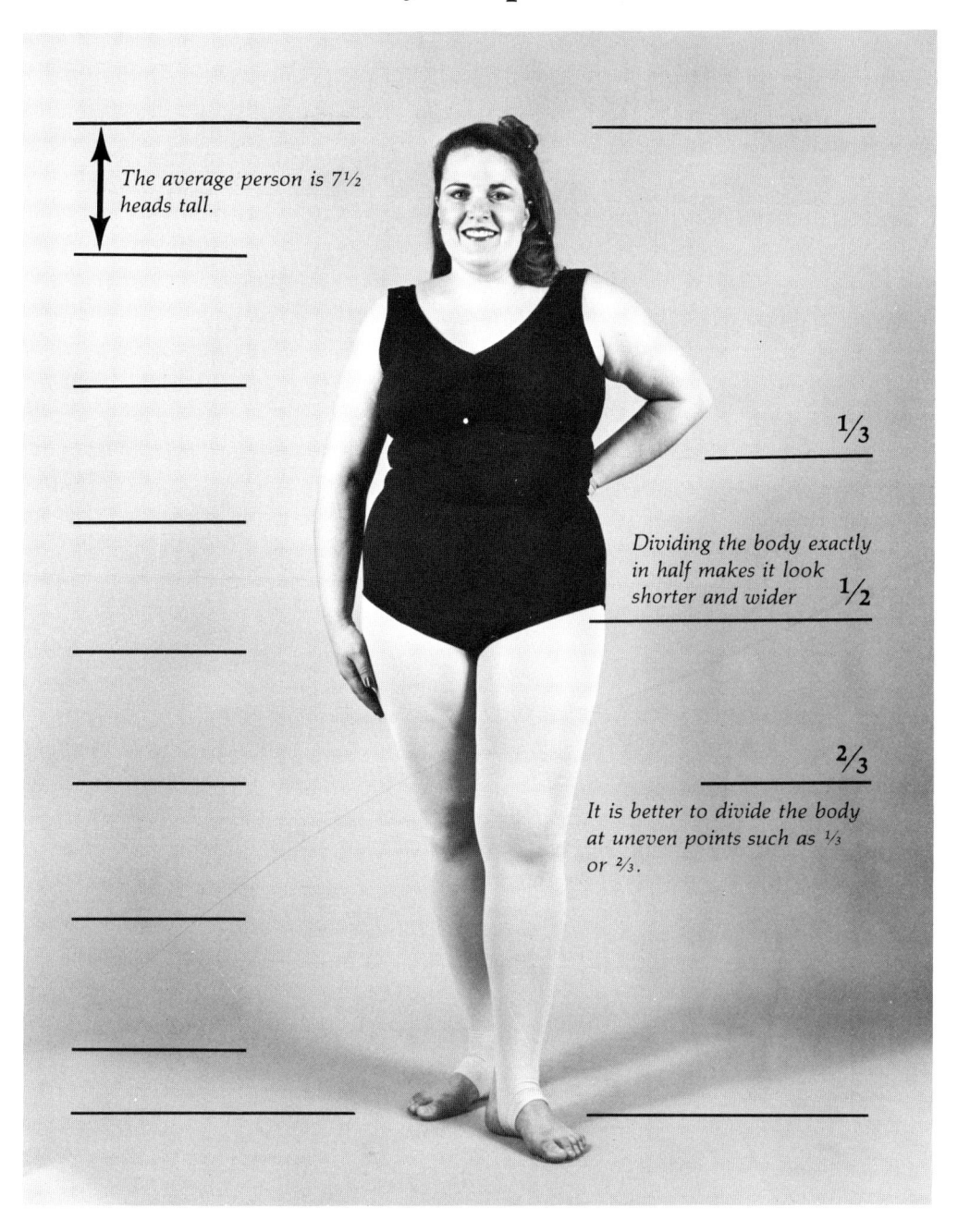

The average person is 7½ heads tall.

⅓

Dividing the body exactly in half makes it look shorter and wider ½

⅔

It is better to divide the body at uneven points such as ⅓ or ⅔.

Big & Beautiful

look shorter and wider. Divide your height again, this time by thirds, and find these two points on your body. Dividing your body into thirds is more pleasing than dividing it exactly in half. Horizontal breaks at the one-third and the two-thirds point can be interesting and flattering. This is also true of proportion within a design. Measure from the shoulder to the hem of a garment, and divide this measurement in half and then in thirds. Dividing the garment exactly in half has the same effect as dividing your body. You can achieve better proportion by emphasizing the one-third or two-thirds points and garment.

Other areas of proportion you should consider are:

1. The length of a skirt or blouse relative to your height and width.

2. Where the waistline falls relative to the length of the dress and your height.

3. The width of a skirt's flare relative to the shoulder line and/or sleeve.

4. Where the jacket hem falls relative to the length of the look and your height.

5. The width of belts, bows, and sashes relative to the scale of your outfit and the total look.

6. The size and spacing of decorations relative to your height and the length of the garment.

7. The size and spacing of details, such as buttons.

8. The spacing of pleats or tucks.

9. The relation of the yoke to the look of the garment.

10. Differing lengths and fullnesses of jackets and skirts to avoid an unflattering boxy effect.

Photo courtesy of Lady Annabelle Lingerie, Inc.

Chapter 7

DEVELOPING A PERSONAL STYLE

I hope you're getting new perspective on your image potential. Image development works, and it isn't as complicated as you might think. Any task is easier when you break it into manageable steps. Now it's time to put all the parts together. You've learned about fashion, balance, and the elements and principles of design. It's time to add your own personal style. To make your image unique, you have to express your personal style.

Have you been working on the role and goal exercises in Chapter 4? Do you know what image you want to project for each of your roles and goals? If you're still undecided, you should work on visualizing yourself in different roles. Visualization helps you think more clearly and lets you focus your energies. Find a comfortable position. Close your eyes and imagine a blank movie screen. The more clearly you see the screen, the more successful your visualization exercise will be. Project a picture of yourself on the screen. Notice what you are wearing and doing. Does the picture represent what you look like now? Does it represent what you want to look like? Pay attention to details. If the image fades, recreate the screen and try again. Each time you repeat the exercise, try to see a sharper, more detailed picture. The more realistic the visualization, the better chance you have of making it a reality.

VISUALIZATION EXERCISE 1

Visualize your face. Now clear your mental screen and select one role and one goal from the exercise in Chapter 4. Visualize the image that best fits that role and that goal. Spend a few minutes thinking about this picture—pretend you're looking in a mirror. Don't worry about what size you imagine your body to be. Instead, concentrate on the specifics of the image. Look for the essence, or mood, or the visualized image; we can translate the visualization to reality later. Clear your mental screen again, and recreate the image you just visualized, but this time, superimpose the first picture of your face. Don't be surprised if nothing particular comes to mind. We've been robbed of our right to look good for so long that many of us have stopped dreaming. Keep at it. You may have to repeat this exercise several times before you're satisfied.

VISUALIZATION EXERCISE 2

Look through newspapers and magazines for pictures that represent the image you'd like to project, and cut out the ones that appeal to you. What message does this image convey? Why do you like it? Why do you want to look like the model in the picture? What goal or role does it represent for you? What aspect of your personality or lifestyle does it portray? Is the image part of you now or is it something you'd like to achieve? Does that particular image convey power, sexuality, maturity, or nurturing?

Close your eyes and visualize the picture you've cut out. Superimpose your face on the image. How do you feel about this combination? What aspects of the visualization do you like? What aspects make you uncomfortable? Are fatphobia stereotypes the only things preventing you from achieving this image? What other problems or feelings will you have to deal with before you'll feel comfortable expressing the image you really want?

It may seem silly to sit around daydreaming, but visualization is a valuable tool. Practice these two exercises several times a day. You can do them whenever you have five or ten minutes to spare. After you have a clear mental picture of the image that is right for one goal and role, move on to another. When you feel comfortable with all the goal and role images on your list, you're ready to turn fantasy into reality.

Study the newspaper and magazine pictures you have selected for your Visualization Exercise 2. Compare the clothing style and details in the picture to the charts on the next 4 pages that classify various designs as **yin** or **yang**. Answer the following questions:

1. What attitude is being expressed? yin yang combination
2. What is the basic clothing style? yin yang combination
3. What does the hairstyle express? yin yang combination
4. What do the clothing details express? yin yang combination
5. What do the accessories express? yin yang combination
6. What does the body language express? yin yang combination
7. What overall expression does the look convey? yin yang combination
8. What is the apparent goal of this look?
9. What roles would this look satisfy?
10. What aspects of my personality and lifestyle does this look express.

Review your **yin-yang** evaluation from Chapter 4. Do you still agree with the answers you selected? If you're having second thoughts, revise the evaluation to reflect the new image you'd like to project. Do you see now that **yin** and **yang** are rather subjective terms, because an outfit can be Yin on one person and Yang on another. Since we're dealing with **your** image, you have to define each term for yourself. There are no right or wrong answers, but do try to be consistent.

Yin Styles Clothing

Style

108

Yang Styles Clothing

Big & Beautiful

109

Yin Styles — Accessories and Details

Necklines and collars

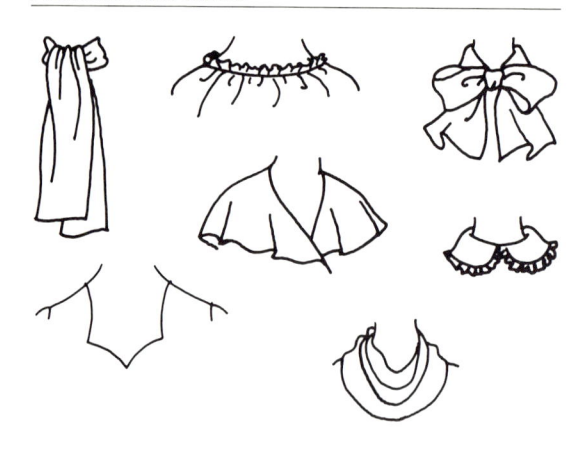

Sleeves

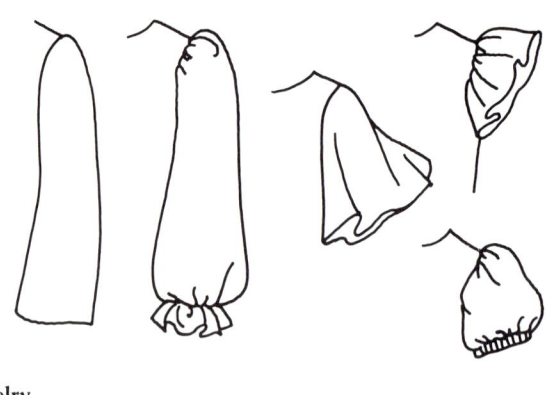

Hats and belts

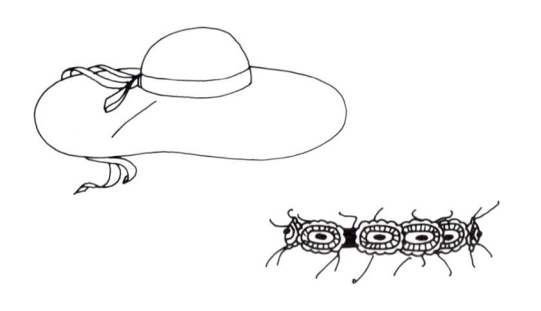

Jewelry

Handbags

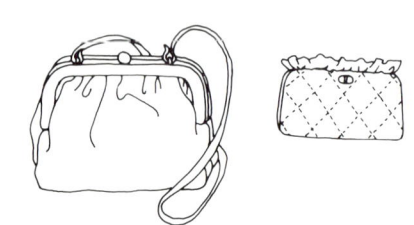

Footwear

Style

110

Yang Styles Accessories and Details

Necklines and collars

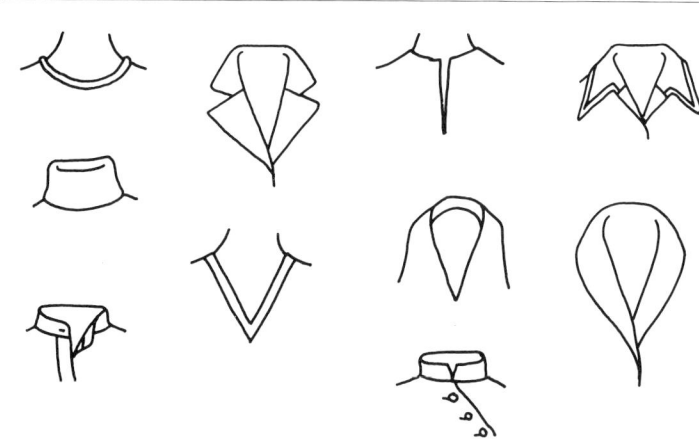

Sleeves

Hats and belts

Jewelry

Handbags

Footwear

Big & Beautiful

VISUALIZATION EXERCISE 3

Dress the image you visualized in Exercise 2 in your favorite outfit. Slowly go over the ten image questions, and label each part of the outfit as **yin**, **yang**, or a combination of both. Visualize and question each outfit you dress your visualized image in. Now visualize those outfits you never seem to wear, and ask yourself the image questions. How do your answers differ from these answers about the outfits you like? How do they compare with your self-evaluation in Chapter 4? Which clothes best match your personality, goals, and roles? Which outfits make your physical image look balanced. Are your natural clothing preferences expressed by your wardrobe? If the clothes in your closet don't match the image you want, it's time to overhaul your wardrobe.

These exercises should give you a better idea of whether the clothes in your wardrobe now will fit with your desired image. But, if we're going to identify ways to improve your image, we'll need a more precise picture. We'll begin our evaluation by looking at basic clothing styles. Observe the silhouette of each garment in your closet, disregarding for the moment color, texture, decorations, and details. If you run into a problem classifying some of the clothes, refer to the **yin–yang** style chart. When I did this exercise, I grouped my clothes into three categories. **Yang** clothes made up about 50 percent of my wardrobe, combination clothes made up about 35 percent, and the other 15 percent were yin clothes. I compared the results to my evaluation. I found my wardrobe was consistent with my preferences and current roles, but I didn't have enough **yin** clothing to express my goals and physical image.

To solve that problem, I could concentrate on buying **yin** clothing over the next few months, or I could focus my attention on the details of my image. Look at the **yin–yang** chart again. Compare those image details to your usual look. Do you favor **yin** hairstyles and accessories? Do the clothing details, such as trim and buttons, reflect a definite **yang** preference? Are you putting **yang**-style makeup on a **yin** face? The answers to these questions will help you fine tune your image.

Instead of investing in **yin** clothing, I added more **yin** details to balance my image. I bought a long strand of pearls, an antique necklace and earring set, and a Victorian-style lace blouse. I experimented with softer hairstyles. With the new **yin** accessories and a new hairstyle, I felt confident my wardrobe was balanced. Once you've developed a balanced image, it's easier to adjust it when you get a new job or determine new goals for yourself.

You're on your way to becoming an image designer. Professional designers have been able to create an almost infinite array of designs from this rather limited variety of necklines, sleeves, and collar styles. Now that you understand how designers create designs, you can do it, too. Just change the length or shape of a skirt, select a different sleeve style or neckline, and you've created a new look. The only tools missing from your new image-building kit are color and texture. Color and texture are complicated subjects. Thanks to the increasing popularity of color analysis, people are becoming aware of what a powerful tool color can be. People who sew know the look of a pattern can be entirely changed just by using different fabric. The concepts of **yin** and **yang** also apply to color and texture.

There are two kinds of texture, visual and tactile. Visual texture refers to surface enrichment, such as prints, that don't actually change the feel of the fabric. Tactile texture changes the feel and look of a fabric. Velvet and corduroy are fabrics with definite tactile texture. **Yin**-textured fabrics are smooth, shiny, light, airy, transparent, or lacy. **Yang**-textured fabrics are rough, dull, heavy, opaque, stiff, or sleek. The reason some garments look funny is that the designer has tried to combine a **yin** fabric with a **yang** design, or vice versa. This is a common problem for beginning seamstresses. Imagine a tight, tailored skirt made of chiffon, or a ruffled blouse made out of corduroy. The styles and textures don't mix.

Before you do any more image-building, you should know the difference between rayon and acrylic? If you don't, it's time to take a trip to your local fabric store. In today's world of wonder fabrics, you need to know what you're buying so you know how to take care of it. Even if you hate to sew, you still need to know something about fabrics, and fabric stores are regular libraries. Take an hour to browse through one. Almost all fabrics have care instructions and contents information printed on the ends of the bolt. Feel the fabric. See how it drapes. Read the information and study any display garments. Would you use that fabric to make that kind of a garment? Flip through the pattern books and see if you can find any other styles that would look good if made from that fabric. Most patterns list suggested fabrics, so check your guesses. Make a game of guessing the fiber content. You may be fooled. Polyester can feel so much like silk or wool that only a chemical test could tell them apart. Familiarizing yourself with fabrics will help you shop for ready-to-wear clothes.

As I've said, the look of a design can be totally changed by the fabric used. Full designs usually look best if made with soft fabrics. Using a soft fabric in a tailored garment can make it look skimpy and wilted. Tailored clothes look best if made with fabrics with natural body. Top stitching, pleats, and pockets usually work best if used on fabrics with body. Remember the rules about balance when you select fabric. If you want to buy a circular skirt made out of velvet, be sure you want to add weight to the lower part of your body. If not, a velvet A-line skirt might be a better choice.

Now, for the element that can mean an instant wardrobe improvement—color. Before we can use color with confidence, we have to know the why and how it affects people. Color evokes emotional and physical responses. When you're "seeing red," "feeling blue," or "green with envy," you're experiencing the full impact of color. Color goes straight to the heart.

Visualize the color red. What do you think of? Danger? Excitement? Sexuality? How about blue? Blue usually makes me think of a peaceful, shimmering mountain lake. What do the colors yellow, black, white, and green make you think of? Some of your responses will be on personal experience, but most of your reactions are shared by almost everyone. Another example of the universal significance of color is the surprising number of cultures, past and present, that have used the healing power of color. Some psychics claim the ability to tell what a person's physical and mental condition is by the colors of that person's aura. Wouldn't it be nice if, the next time you had a headache, you could tie a blue ribbon around your head instead of taking an aspirin?

Before you dismiss this claim as the product of a primitive mind, you should know that science has found evidence confirming the power of color. Some scientists have had limited success using colored lights to cure certain ailments. They think the color waves, which are part of the electromagnetic spectrum, somehow stimulate certain electrical impulses that, in turn, cause the brain to react in predictable ways. This might explain why red, whose waves are the longest on the spectrum, tends to excite people and why blue, with the shortest wave length, tends to calm people.

Now you know that color is a powerful magic, so how do you use it to improve your image? Before I learned to use color appropriately, I relied on prejudice, emotional preference, whim, and fatphobia stereotypes to guide me in selecting colors. My ignorance about color ruined my poor husband's image. Like most wives, shortly after we were married my husband delegated the buying of his clothes to me. I gradually changed his soft blue, burgundy, gray, and navy wardrobe into rich browns, creamy beiges, and soft golds—colors I prefer. As the colors in his wardrobe improved according to my taste, his coloring got worse. After he took a trip to the doctor and I visited a color consultant, I realized I'd been dressing him in the colors that were right for me, not him. He looked like he had a bad case of jaundice. After a quick closet cleaning and a shopping trip, he looked as handsome and healthy as ever.

So how do you avoid the wrong colors? Have your colors analyzed. The art and science of color analysis isn't new. Artists have long known that skintone is a combination of melanin, keratin, and hemoglobin. Melanin gives the skin its brown tones, keratin gives the yellow tones, and hemoglobin gives the red tones. Several hundred years ago, Robert Dior created the Color Key I and Color Key II system of classifying skin tone. He found that skin tone, like all colors, can be classified as either warm or cool. Yellowish undertones mean warm skin color; pink or blueish undertones mean cool coloring.

Over the years, the color key system has been expanded and changed. Someone decided there were three basic skin tones: pink, peach, and orange. Then a German art teacher found four skin tones that were derived from the four seasons of the year. On the West Coast, "What's your season?" has replaced "What's your sign?" as cocktail party chatter. That doesn't mean color analysis isn't a valid way to select complimentary colors. Color analysis is based on the theory that certain groups of color waves vibrate in harmony with each other, like the notes in a song. Skin tone is just one note in the song of color harmony. Though some color consultants claim only highly trained specialists can analyze someone's colors, the average person manages to select 50–75 percent of their wardrobe in the right color family. With a little training, you can approach 100 percent accuracy.

This discussion is not meant as a substitute for a personal color analysis or further study. Reading Carole Jackson's **Color Me Beautiful** (Acropolis Books Ltd., 1980) would be an excellent next step in your study of color. You'll have to judge the value of color analysis for yourself. I started using the following system to help people long before color analysis was in vogue.

What is the most important thing to consider when selecting a color? Your hair? Your eyes? What colors it goes with? These are all important considerations, but the single most important thing in selecting the majority of your colors is your skin tone. Surprised? I was, too. When you think about it, it makes sense. After all, skin is what you have the most of. The second important consideration is your hair color. The color your eyes is the least important consideration in choosing your colors. These rules are not carved in stone, though.

We'll use a very basic system to classify skin tone colors. As we said before, skin has either warm or cool undertones. We can further classify skin tone by its intensity. If a woman with pale blonde hair and delicate coloring had warm skin undertones, she would be classified as warm/fair. If she had cool skin undertones, she would be a cool/fair. Our model,

Alicia, is an excellent example of a cool/fair. A black woman with black hair and dark eyes, like our model Teddi, would be considered a cool/rich. If Teddi's skin had golden undertones rather than pink undertones, she would have been considered a warm/rich.

You can analyze your colors alone or in a group. I find that working in a group makes it easier, because it's easier to decide what someone else's colors are. Besides, it's usually more fun. For best results, select a room lit by natural sunlight. Artificial light can change the test results. Don't wear makeup when you conduct the test, because the wrong color foundation can change the results. The person who's being analyzed should cover their clothes with an old white sheet. This will cut down on color confusion.

Collect color samples of true, clear pink; soft, pastel pink; dark pink: medium-value orange; pastel orange; and red-orange. Make sure the samples aren't muted, grayed, dusty, too harsh, or too bright. You can use almost anything as a sample, as long as it's the right color. I've used towels, sheets, fabric, scarves, clothing, and colored paper.

To give you an idea of how my color analysis system works, I'll use an example from a group I worked with several months ago. I had Sandy cover her hair because she'd just colored it and wasn't happy with the results. We started with the medium pink and orange samples. I held the pink sample up to her face. Her skin looked pale and cloudy. The lines around her mouth, nose, and eyes were accentuated. The new blemishes she had stood out. When you looked at her from across the room, you noticed the color before you noticed her face.

Next, I held the medium orange sample near her face. It was amazing how her face seemed to brighten up. The orange made her complexion look creamy and clear. You hardly noticed any circles, shadows, or lines. She instantly looked healthier, even without makeup. Sandy definitely had warm skin undertones. I recommended she go back to a hair color a shade nearer her natural color, since nature gives us the right hair and eye color for our skin tones. Sandy had lightened her strawberry blonde hair to ash blonde, and the cool undertones of the ash blonde hair were fighting with the warm undertones of her skin.

Now we wanted to determine the intensity of her skin tone. I held the light and dark orange samples next to her skin. The dark orange sample looked alright, but the light orange sample made her sparkle. If the dark orange sample had looked the best, she would have been a warm/rich. Since the medium and light samples did the most for her appearance, we knew she had a warm/fair skin tone.

Our second volunteer was Sandy's complete opposite. Cheryl had straight black hair and dark brown eyes. We started with the medium orange and pink samples. The orange sample drained the color from her face. The pink sample looked 100 percent better. We then tried the dark and light pink samples. The light pink sample looked good, but the dark pink looked even better. We tried the light orange and dark orange samples just for comparison. The group's unanimous opinion was that Cheryl had a cool/rich skin tone.

- Warm/fair skin tones look best with the medium and light orange samples.
- Warm/rich skin tones look best with the medium and dark orange samples.
- Cool/fair skin tones look best with the medium and light pink samples.
- Cool/rich skin tones look best with the medium and dark pink samples.

Unless they are very fair, most people can usually wear the medium value of a color. If the medium samples seem to overpower anyone in your group, try the lighter samples. A person has the same basic undertone throughout life but the intensity may change due to age or tanning. Your colors may be hard to find at times because fashion has color cycles. Warm colors were popular until recently. We are now entering a period of cool color popularity. If you are a cool/fair and cool/rich, buy now, because certain colors may be harder to find later on.

This is a brief summary of the colors best for each skin tone. Don't be surprised if your favorite color isn't included. You may look great in it, but then again, it may be best to enjoy your favorite color on your walls, not next to your face.

Cool/Rich Skin Tone

Think of dramatic contrast when you think about the colors right for you. You have the only skin tone that is complimented by pure white and black. These colors are too harsh for the other skin tones, but they are the perfect dramatic highlights for your striking coloring. Any shade of gray is an excellent neutral color for you. Avoid browns and tans, except for taupe. Navy is another great basic color for you. The blues you select should be clear—true blue, royal blue, or icy blue. Hot turquoise and pale aqua can look good on some cool/rich skin tones. Greens, like the blues, should be true and rich, or pale and icy. Avoid orange. Pinks are among your best colors, but lean towards the extremes. Most of your pinks should range from medium to deep. Toss in a few light pinks for balance.

Cool/Fair Skin Tone

The colors for cool/fair skin tones should be grayed and relatively light. Dark, strong colors will overpower the fragile coloring of this skin tone. Soft white, rose-beige, and rose brown are good basic colors for you. All blues, from light to medium, including grayed navy, will flatter your coloring. For the best effects, make sure your greens tend toward the blue side. Avoid black, pure white, orange, and most browns. Light to medium pinks will make your skin glow.

Warm/Rich Skin Tone

Creamy, golden colors are key to your color success. Stay away from gray, black, navy, and pink. Warm whites, beiges, tans, and just about any brown, are your best basic colors. Warm blues, such as teal blue and periwinkle blue, won't fight with your coloring the way cool blues will. Greens from turquoise to forest, should definitely be in your wardrobe in large quantities. Oranges, from deep peach to rust, are another wardrobe must.

Warm/Fair Skin Tone

Be careful not to overpower your delicate coloring. Pure white and black are definitely out. Ivory, creamy beige, golden browns, and warm gray make great basics for you. You can wear blues ranging from light navy to light royal blue to periwinkle blue. Turquoise and aqua are also good colors for you. When you select greens, think of the yellow tints of new spring grass. Keep your oranges on the light to pink side. Apricot, salmon, and coral colors will highlight your rosy complexion. Unlike the warm/rich skin tones, you can wear some pinks, but you may have to experiment to find the right peachy pink for you.

All these pretty, new colors won't do you any good if you can't overcome the fatphobia stereotypes about color. Those people who tell you dark, drab colors will make you look smaller don't know what they're talking about. Dark, ugly colors make you look older, dowdier, and frumpier. They may make you invisible, but they certainly don't make you look smaller. Vibrant, attractive colors make you feel wonderful, and they make you look younger and more fashionable. Attractive colors make you look sensational, not bigger. If you're not used to wearing lively colors, add them to your wardrobe slowly. When you start hearing the compliments, you'll be glad you did. I shouldn't say ugly when referring to colors. There aren't any ugly colors, just colors that are improperly used. This seems to be a major shortcoming of color analysis. Some color consultants tell you about all those pretty colors, but they don't tell you how to use them effectively.

When I'm in doubt about what colors to wear, I rely on the color schemes I learned in art class. The safest scheme is monochromatic, which means all the shades and tints of a color plus a neutral, like black, white, or gray. An example of monochromatic scheme would be an outfit using red, pink, black and white. Monochromatic color schemes can be dramatic or boring. You should vary the texture and value the lightness or darkness of a color of the color to keep your outfit interesting.

Another conservative standby is the adjacent color scheme. Imagine a color wheel—warm colors like orange, red, and yellow are on the top; cool colors like blue, green, and purple are on the bottom. An adjacent color scheme uses one color and the colors on either side of it. Blue, blue-green, and green form an adjacent color scheme. Be sure to vary the value of the colors to avoid a boring combination.

The complementary and split-complementary color schemes are more daring approaches to color use. Complementary color scheme has the highest level of contrast. Complementary colors are on opposite sides of the color wheel. Blue and orange, red and green, and yellow and purple are examples of complementary color schemes. Using an equal amount of two complementary colors doesn't usually achieve the best result. Seventy-five percent of one color and 25 percent of its complement would be a better mix.

A split-complementary color scheme consists of a color and the two colors on either side of its complement. Red, blue, and yellow is the most common split-complementary scheme. Yellow, orange, and green is another possibility. The more complex the color wheel, the more colors you can make combinations from. Many art supply stores carry color wheels marked with the various color scheme combinations. This is not an art lesson, but if you don't know how to use your new colors in interesting ways, what good are they?

Here are five simple rules that will help you use color effectively.

1. The smaller the area, the brighter the color. The larger the area, the duller the color.

2. Small, bright areas of color should be used to draw attention to the area you want to emphasize.

3. Never use equal parts of a highly contrasting color combination.

4. The dominant color will set the mood.

5. Texture will affect color.

The first rule is very important in terms of balance. That is, a small area of bright color balances a large area of dull color. Repeating a color several times in an outfit is another way to achieve balance, but be careful how you repeat a color. Don't wear eye shadow the same color as your eyes. It won't emphasize your eyes and balance your look. A sharp contrast can sometimes be more effective than repeating a color or colors. Blue eye shadow on blue eyes can make your eyes seem faded by comparison. Brown or gray shadow might be a better choice. Don't forget that color combinations can look different from a distance. I once saw a lady walking down the street wearing what looked like a kelly green skirt with a shocking pink blouse. "Poor thing," I thought, "she could really use some help." When she got closer, I could see that the pink blouse had small, kelly green stripes. Up close, the combination was interesting. From a distance, it made you wonder.

I buy my clothes in color units. The more expensive an item, the more basic the color I choose. I save wild colors for accessories that I can afford to discard when they go out of fashion. When I'm planning to add a new color unit to my wardrobe, I first consider the color groups I already own. If I already have brown and rust color units, I'd add an off-white unit so all the colors could be mixed and matched. We'll talk more about building these color units in the next chapter, but I wanted you to see that there's a method to my madness.

It's time to get down to the personality aspects of color. **Yin** and **yang** work for color, too. People with strong contrasts in their coloring will look best in strongly contrasting color schemes. People with little contrast in their coloring should stick to color schemes with little contrast.

If you are a loud, outgoing person, bright, lively colors will best express your personality. If you are the quiet, conservative type, soft, delicate colors will make you more comfortable. Strong color contrast suggests active, dynamic characters. Closely related color schemes suggest a relaxed, person. Use the following guidelines to determine whether a color is **yin** or **yang**, and then apply the results as you have with the other exercises in this chapter.

A **yin** color or a **yin** combination of colors is:

- Bright and true
- Middle value or medium intensity
- Strong value contrast
- Strong color scheme (complementary and split-complementary)

A **yang** color or **yang** combination of colors is:

- Darker shades
- Dull
- Little value contrast
- Monochromatic or adjacent color schemes
- Dominantly cool harmonies.

Rough textures can make colors look darker. Smooth, shiny textures make colors look lighter. Yellow, yellow-green, and violet are the hardest colors to wear, because they tend to reflect harshly on the skin.

We have just covered a lot of information, so I suggest you reread this chapter. Don't miss anything; this is an important chapter in your image development. You are now ready to face the final challenge in developing your physical image—a shopping trip. Now you have to learn how to become a smart image shopper so you can put all your newfound knowledge to work.

Photo courtesy of YOUNG STUFF a division of Stout Sportswear Group.

What Are Yin and Yang People?

The Yin Personality
Active, outgoing and feminine types, *yin* clothing should be soft, lacey, flowing, fluffy, comfortable, informal and unstructured.

The Yang Personality
Dynamic, powerful and assertive types, *yang* clothing should be tailored, sophisticated, elegant, dramatic, formal and structured.

Yin *and* yang *are ancient Chinese terms for the opposites that make up a whole. They are used in this book to show the opposites in personality and style that make up each person. Though everyone is a combination of both* yin *and* yang, *one personality type usually dominates.*

Plate A

What Are Yin and Yang Colors?

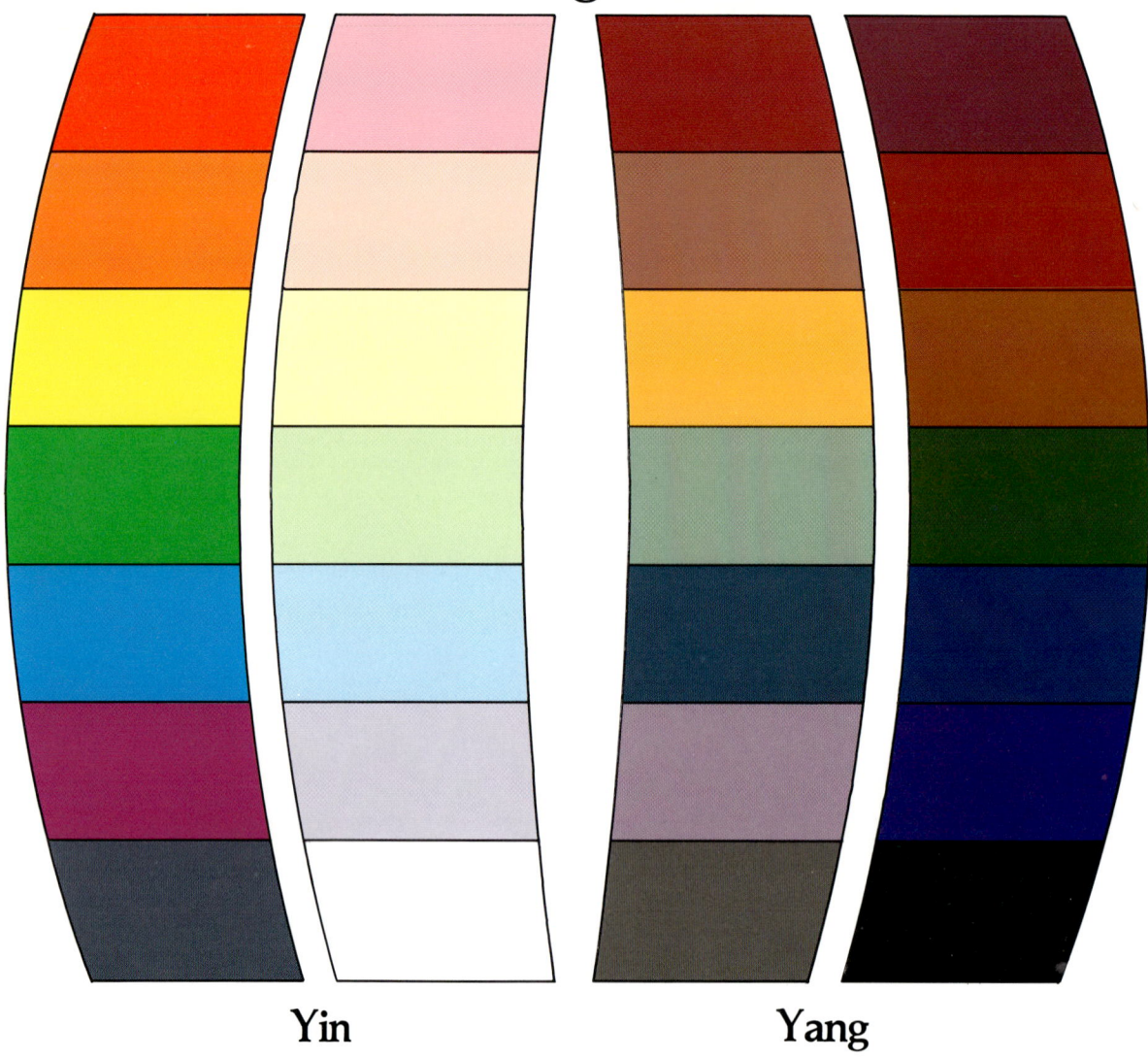

Yin   **Yang**

*C*olor can reveal much about your personality. Once you've determined whether you are predominantly a Yin or a Yang, you'll want to know which colors will best reflect your image. This color chart shows the soft, delicate, bright clear warm colors that reveal *yin* characteristics and the dull, dark, cool colors that project *yang* traits. Read Chapter 7 for more information on how you can use color in your life.

Plate B

What Are Yin and Yang Styles?

Yin   Yang

*S*ince Yins are often informal, active, outgoing and feminine types, their clothing should be too. And, since Yangs are dynamic, dignified dramatic, so should their wardrobes be. This chart shows which styles reflect yin traits and which reflect yang characteristics.

Plate
C

Which Color Is Better?

Alicia in a *yin* color

Alicia in a *yang* color

*A*licia, too, looks much more vibrant and alive in the yang and complementary makeup. The pale yin color and no makeup does nothing to enhance her natural skin-tone, hair and eye coloring.

Plate
D

Which Style Is Better?

Alicia in a *yin* style

Alicia in a *yang* style

Here Alicia demonstrates how different are the images of yin and yang *clothing styles. She can project a sophisticated assured business look in her yang clothing, or soften her image with ruffles and a less severe hairstyle to look more approachable. In her yang outfit she wears darker makeup to dramatize her authority.*

Which Color Is Better?

Teddi in a *yin* color

Teddi in a *yang* color

Here you can see that Teddi really looks better in the vivid, dramatic rose yang color and complementary makeup. She looks washed out in the yin color and no makeup. Color really does make a difference. Sometimes it is difficult to see on yourself, but on another person a color change can be dramatic.

Plate F

Which Style Is Better?

Teddi in a *yin* style

Teddi in a *yang* style

Neither. Teddi can wear either a yang or a yin outfit, depending on the mood she wants to create. She looks great in either because they are in her beautiful **yang** rose. Notice how ruffles, pearls and a soft asymmetrical hairstyle make her look very romantic. The balanced **yang** look is much more tailored and formal.

Plate G

Which Color Is Better?

Kelly in a *yin* color

Kelly in a *yang* color

Kelly really looks better in the soft, pink yin *color and makeup. The* yang *color overpowers her delicate coloring. Kelly has a more delicate* yin *personality that definitely shows up better in the less dramatic colors of the* yin *spectrum.*

Plate
H

Which Style Is Better?

Kelly in a *yin* style

Kelly in a *yang* style

Here Kelly shows how she can effectively wear either the soft *yin* sweater and hairstyle and the more dramatic, stylized *yang* outfit. She looks good in both, but creates a very different image in each: one demure, the other assertive. In other words, you can change your image when you change your clothes. Read Chapter 8 for more of the language of fashion.

Plate I

Wardrobe Plan: A Sporty Yin

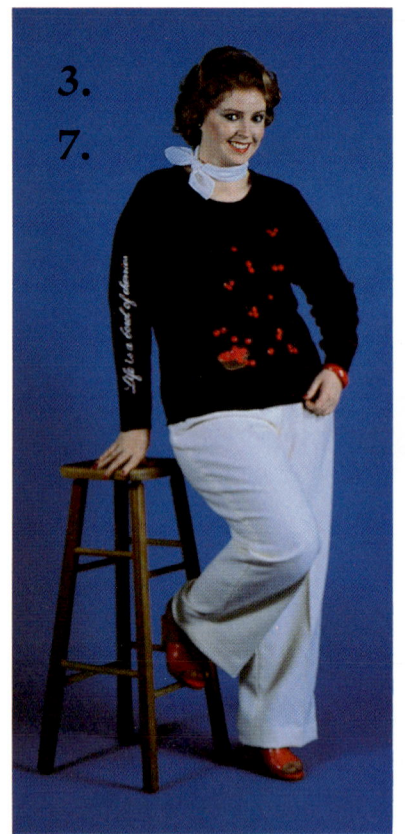

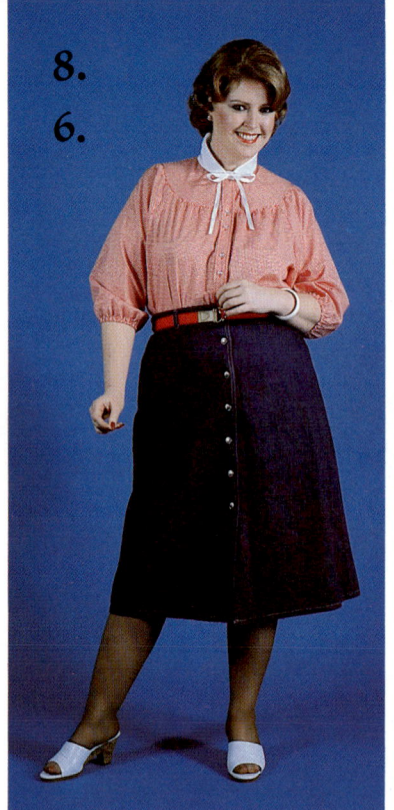

Barbara wears a sporty yin wardrobe in these pictures. Eight pieces of clothing—Variety of casual outfits emerge from 1. a spring green bomber jacket; 2. a clear red cotton shirt; 3. a navy blue and red patterned sweater; 4. a pair of navy blue shorts; 5. a light blue and patterned reversible wraparound skirt; 6. a navy denim skirt; 7. a pair of white tailored pants; 8. and a red-and-white plaid shirt.

Plate J

Wardrobe Plan: A Soft Yang

1.
5.
7.

1.
7.
4.

6.
8.

1.
2.
4.
5.
6.
3.
7.
8.

Here Linda models a soft yang wardrobe consisting of just eight pieces of clothing: 1. a collarless, off-white jacket; 2, 3. a 2-piece gray suit; 4. a gray, pink and cream print blouse; 5. a tailored pink shirt; 6. a burgundy knit top; 7. an off-white stitched-pleat skirt; 8. and a burgundy knit A-line skirt. All of the elements are classic, tailored yang styles.

Plate K

*F*ind your own style. Yin and yang are useful concepts in defining fashion. Often the most interesting wardrobes are made up of a combination of both. Above you see a dress in a yin style and a yin pattern. The color of the dress and the belt are yang. The yin dress is made more assertive and dramatic with these yang components. The outfit is a complete and harmonious combination of both styles.

Plate L

Chapter 8

THE LANGUAGE OF FASHION

I hope you are beginning to see how important image development is in the fight against fatphobia. By developing a personal style, you are getting in touch with the unique person that is you. How do you project your image and remain within the boundaries of current fashion? Come to think of it, how do you figure out what the fashion industry is going to come up with next? It sometimes seems the only reason people follow fashion is because it's like the weather, always changing. If we're going to become smart image shoppers, we need a fundamental understanding of how the fashion industry works.

I learned how fickle fashion is and has been one summer in Marin, California. Each summer, a group of entertainers in Marin recreates a complete Renaissance village. Actors and actresses attend classes for months to prepare themselves for the seven-weekend event. As many as 2000 performers research and invent completely authentic characters to become "members of the shire."

As novice magicians, my husband and I thought this festival would be a good place to practice our craft and maybe make some money. In the sizzling August heat, we dressed as if we were in balmy England. It was like stepping through the looking glass back to a time when big was considered beautiful. In Renaissance England, an extra layer of fat was welcome insulation from the cold. Only the richest men could afford a full barn and a fat wife.

The theater company was so determined to be authentic that thin women were required to wear special padding. Can you imagine skinny women wearing hot, heavy padding so they could have what we have all the time? For once, they envied me. The company actors were so believable in their lust for plump ladies that the people attending the fair caught the "big is beautiful" spirit. I was amazed to see large lasses getting more attention than skinny wenches. One big woman made a fortune by tucking an apple into her ample bosom and selling a bite to any young lads who wanted to prove his manhood.

At the end of the fair, I missed the acceptance of my body size. I had to travel back in history before I realized how much society expects women's bodies to change along with the shape of the styles. And we still expect the same changes today. A few seasons ago, fashion magazines featured rosy-cheeked, all-American girls. This season mysterious catlike women are in vogue.

To fit the changing fashion silhouette, the shape of your body has to change, too. During the fifties, women wore girdles to squeeze down to an eighteen inch waistline. During the sixties, women were supposed to look like little boys. Now, if you have legs up to your armpits, no fanny, and you border on six feet tall, you've got it made. You'd have to have your own plastic surgeon to keep up with what's acceptable. Body size and shape is a matter of individual taste. Unfortunately, our tastes change according to the attitudes of the time.

Why can't we love both the ample curves of the new Renaissance women and the trim bodies currently in favor. Is it realistic to expect body size and shape to change each time fashions change? If we all concentrate on developing a personal style, we might be able to break the fashion-body size connection. Once we get over our fear of being different, we can explore each new fashion and judge it according to personal style, our particular set of distinguishing characteristics, and the size and shape of our bodies.

Style refers to any unique design. It may be hard to believe, but there are only three basic clothing styles: straight, bell, or back-fullness.

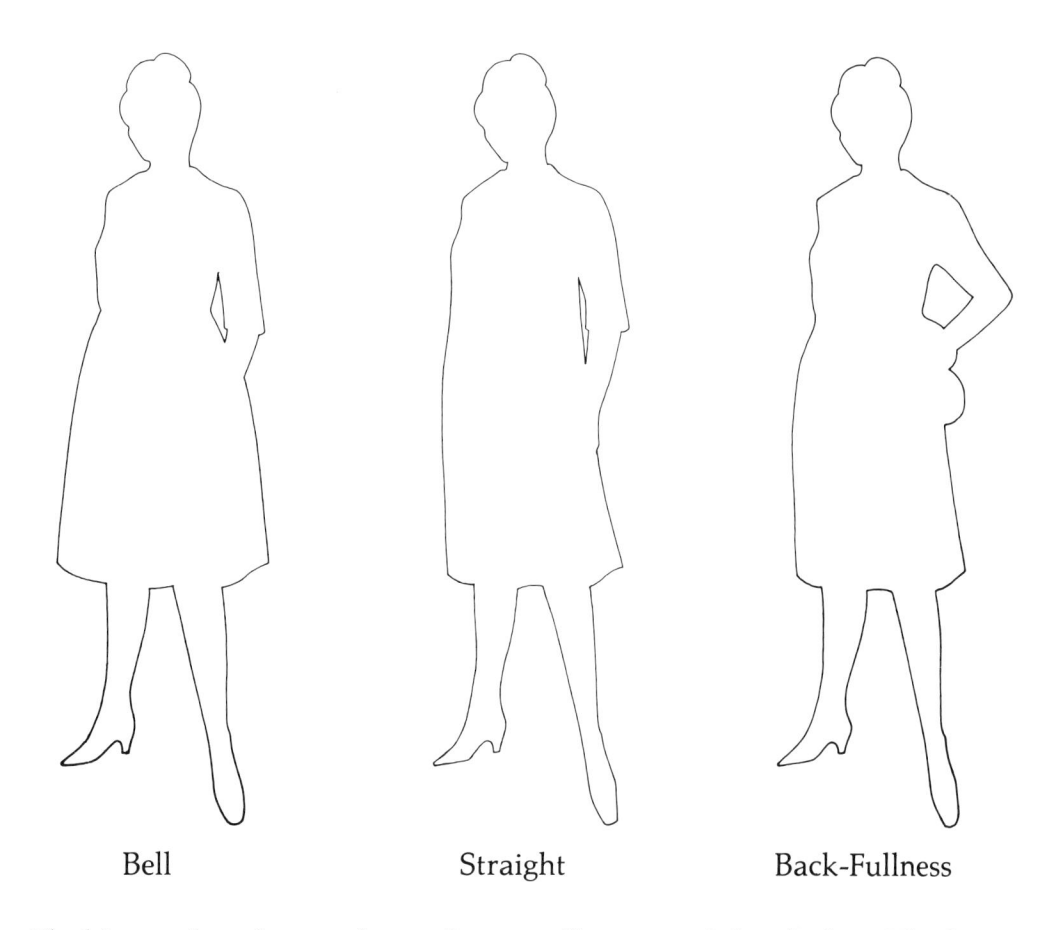

| Bell | Straight | Back-Fullness |

Clothing style refers to the outline or silhouette of the clothes. The basic style, or silhouette, seems to change every thirty to thirty-five years. We are undergoing a basic style change now. The last popular silhouette was the full or bell style skirt. Softly gathered skirts with emphasis at the waist are being replaced by the straight, or tabular, look. Next waistlines will probably drop to hip level and move up under the bustline. Then, waistline emphasis will disappear completely, just as it did in the sixties when the last straight fashion look was popular.

Modern fashion seems to bounce back and forth between the bell and straight silhouettes. Bustles were the last example of a back-fullness craze. The only back-fullness designs I've seen recently were a few wedding and cocktail dresses. Let's hope a back-fullness craze doesn't recur. Can you picture a statuesque woman wearing a bustle and trying to get into a Honda Civic gracefully?

Fashion is a particular style that is popular at a particular time. Today, we have fashion in just about every area of our lives—in cars, kitchen appliances, interior design, and clothing. High fashion is supposed to forecast and promote new trends. Most high fashion, however, is outrageous. It is possible, and highly probable, that you can look both "high fashion" and terrible at the same time.

Fads aren't always fashions. Fads serve a special function. Good fads (yes, there are such things) mix the familiar and the new in a non-threatening way. Fads are a normal, healthy, safe way for the average person to be a little crazy. They can also be annoying. Fads are usually inexpensive and pass more quickly than fashions. When the novelty wears off, you can afford to toss it in the bottom of your closet or sell it at a garage sale. Some fads, like jeans and tee shirts with slogans become so popular that they become fashions.

In addition to the major changes in silhouettes we also have to worry about the fashion and fad cycles in shoes, accessories, hairstyles, and makeup. With so many constantly changing elements its no wonder fashion seems so unpredictable. But it isn't as unpredictable as you think. All you have to do is figure out when the cycles will change. The key to predicting fashion trends is the money supply. **Rule 1:** If fashion cost a lot or people don't have very much money, fashion changes more slowly. When the cash doesn't flow, fashion goes. **Rule 2:** When attitudes become conservative, the range of what is considered acceptable narrows. This is based on the fact that people follow fashion because they don't want to be different. During conservative times, individuality is frowned upon and fashion becomes more narrowly defined and changes more slowly. If the first two rules are true, the blazer you just bought will be fashionable for quite a while. **Rule 3:** Don't expect all fashion trends to be logical. I suppose this is the exception that proves Rules 1 and 2. As long as people buy clothes for looks, not for comfort and protection, fashion will be subject to an occasional attack of the crazies.

All fashion follows the same predictable pattern. Keep in mind that we are talking about a series of overlapping cycles. Each cycle consists of four phases. The first phase is the introduction and the rise in popularity of a new design. This is usually considered the high fashion cycle. In the second phase, the trendsetters adopt the idea. Phase three begins when the average person adapts a version of the trendsetters version of high fashion. In phase four, everyone, including the family dog, is wearing the new look. Sadly, all fashion is doomed to end in excess. When you've noticed a fashion has moved to phase three, it's time to move on to something new.

Both fads and fashions follow the same pattern. The length of time a fad or fashion remains popular depends on its importance, cost, and purpose. Skylab tee shirts didn't last long because the darn thing fell out of the sky too soon. Jewelry fads usually come and go more quickly than fads in shoes. And shoe fads don't last as long as clothing fads. Basic clothing styles are the slowest to change because it's too expensive to revamp your entire wardrobe each year.

You must identify the fashion trendsetters if you're going to second-guess them. What directs the whims of fashion? Since the fashion industry doesn't seem to be overly concerned about reality when it introduces each season's look, who decides? The designers. They're the real fashion fortune-tellers. We're not talking about the designers who have reduced fashion to the level of a cheap publicity stunt. Each season, the fashion circus in Paris and Milan is a good example of fashion exploitation. Designers compete with the most outrageous costumes, trying to catch the eye of the press. This is not to say high fashion is worthless. It does give us something to talk about. If you develop a well-trained eye, you will be able to predict what the average person will be wearing several years from now.

The high fashion of Paris and Milan isn't made for people to wear. At one time, the big European fashion houses used their season premieres to introduce new silhouettes and colors that would eventually filter into everyone's wardrobe. Competition and the economy have turned these shows into media events. While it may be entertaining to watch beanpole women dressed in Star Wars costumes, these shows do nothing to help you plan your working wardrobe. So why do the designers spend thousands of dollars on these outlandish costumes? Most designers survive on their middle-of-the-road merchandise, and anytime they get their name in the paper, it increase their ready-to-wear sales. The real center of fashion is here in the United States: New York. European designers now watch what happens in the New York market because they know their bread-and-butter customer wants clothes to live in, not clothes to be seen in.

Designers in Los Angeles, San Francisco, and Chicago aren't ashamed to admit they design clothes for Ms. Average America. That's where the money is. If we tell them what we want, these American designers are the ones who'll give big women clothes that work. I know it's hard to believe that progress is being made when you still pick up fashion magazines that aren't in touch with your lifestyle. It's discouraging when the stores don't seem to care. We **can** change the industry if we are loud enough and persistent enough.

It's ironic that the real fashion world in America is experiencing what is called the "Europeanization of fashion." Europeanization refers to a return to a classic, continental way of dressing. The classic, continental attitude about dressing is that a few good things worn tastefully are much better than a closet full of mismatched garments. What does this mean to fat Americans? It means we won't have to spend a fortune to look good. We'll be able to buy fewer and better clothes without worrying they will go out of style before they're paid for. We'll save time and money because we'll make fewer mistakes. Once we've carefully selected our basic clothes, we can forget about them, because we know we can express our personal style with inexpensive accessories. After being confused and left out of the fashion picture for so long, it's almost too good to be true.

It's time to prepare for our last challenge in creating our new image. We're going to learn how to shop with a plan. Doing a little homework now will cut down on legwork and frustration later. Don't confuse personal taste with good taste. They aren't always the same thing. Bay Area columnist, Marcy Bachmann, expressed it best, "People seeking status run the risk of having no class, but people with class never even worry about status at all." Part of developing good taste is learning how to buy clothes that are beautiful, appropriate, practical, and becoming.

Only you can decide what you think is beautiful, it's part of your personal style. We can, however, decide what is appropriate, practical, and becoming. We've discussed what styles are becoming for you previously. What styles are practical and appropriate depends on where and when they'll be worn. Return to your analysis of your roles and goals. If your outfit is right for the occasion and the environment, then it's appropriate. If your best buddy right now is your two-year-old, appropriate means something that's going to outlast him. If you're headed up the corporate ladder, what styles are appropriate are dictated by your coworkers. It doesn't matter if you're dressing for the boardroom or the bedroom, as long as you're clear about what is appropriate for your goal.

Ask yourself these questions when you're trying to decide if an outfit is appropriate:

- What is the occasion—school, vacation, sports, or office?
- Where will you wear your outfit—city, country, park, or boardroom?
- What is the climate—cold, foggy, hot, humid, or air-conditioned? etc.
- What are the local customs?
- What are your body requirements?

- What is the message you're trying to convey—sexy, friendly, or aloof?
- What kind of people will be there—young, old, liberal, or conservative?

Even though we don't always dress for comfort and protection, we do generally consider whether a garment is practical. Given the economy, practicality and quality are becoming synonymous. Sometimes we need to put quality on the endangered species list. You can still find quality clothes, but you must be willing to look. Here are some potential problem areas you should examine carefully when you shop for clothes:

Collars: A sloppy, misshapen collar can make a whole outfit look bad. Collars and lapels should be stitched evenly so they fall smoothly. Most collars need interfacing to give them the body so they hang properly.

Buttons and Buttonholes: Buttonholes and the fabric around buttons should never pucker or gap. Buttonholes reinforced with small stitches will last the longest. If the buttonhole or button is unraveling, it won't last through one washing. Don't buy it unless you plan to reinforce both button and buttonhole. It's against the laws of nature for a button to be held on by two threads, so don't even try.

Pockets and Flaps: Make sure all pockets and pocket flaps are even. Who needs lopsided pockets? On quality garments, pockets are reinforced, lined, or finished. Unless you like finding little balls of thread and lint when you're looking for a kleenex, don't compromise on quality.

Cuffs: Cuffs should either be the right length, or they should have enough extra material to allow you to lengthen them. That is, provided you are inclined to tackle such a project. There are all kinds of cuffs on pants and shirts, and they all should be reinforced and neatly stitched.

Seams: If the seams pucker and pull in the store, they will probably always look bad, despite a good ironing. Mistakes made in the factory can seldom be fixed with an iron. Puckered, uneven seams that unravel aren't a good buy, no matter how cheap they are.

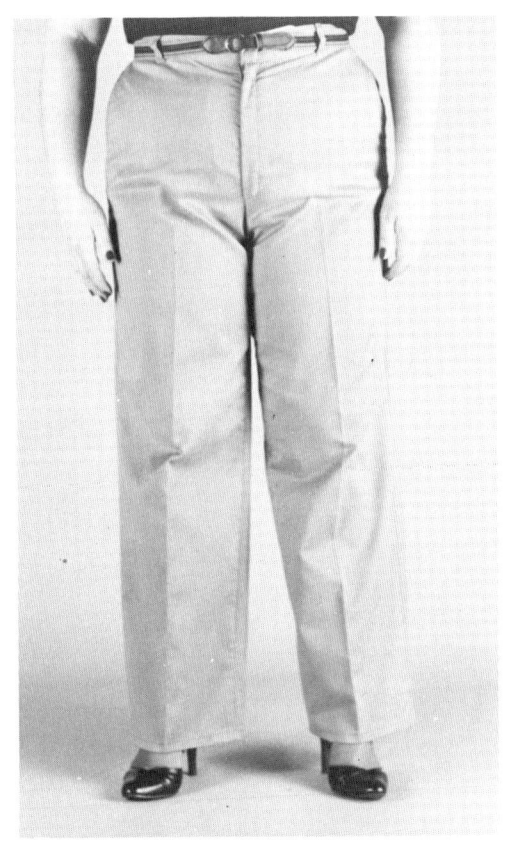

Pants that fit too tightly in the crotch and the hips create an unflattering hemlength and tend to pull forming a "smile."

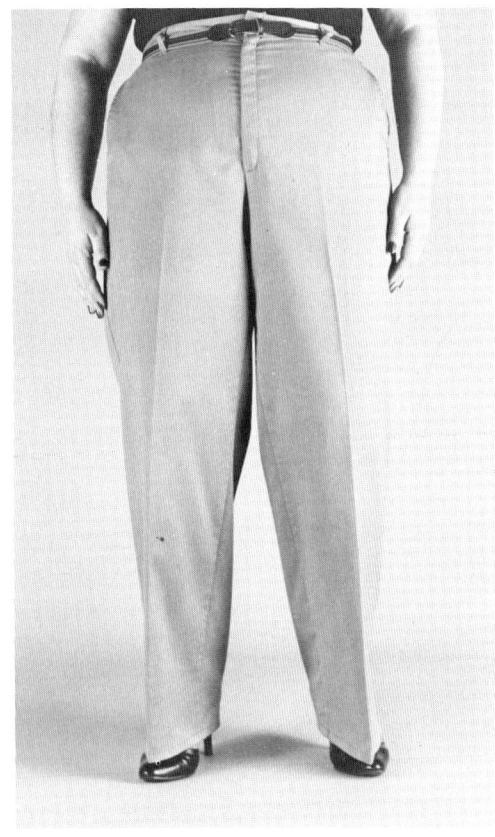

Pants that fit properly don't pull or wrinkle; here, a smooth, streamlined effect is achieved.

Sleeves: The fit of a sleeve is critical to the overall success of your look. Make sure the sleeve cap, or top, is stitched smoothly, free of puckers or pulls. Sleeves that are too tight or too short, or sleeves with droopy shoulder seams will throw your proportion off.

Linings: Linings extend the life of a garment, improve the fit, and reduce wrinkles. They're usually worth the extra expense, if they hang properly. Make sure the lining doesn't pull or droop. The care instructions should be similar to those for the outer garment. I've seen cotton garments lined with fabric that couldn't be washed. Talk about dumb.

Hems: Hems shouldn't pucker or show. I know it is a lot to ask of some manufacturers, but I like my hems sewn with the same color thread as the rest of the garment. I wish manufacturers would stop using lightweight fishing line to hem clothes. It can poke you in the back of the leg when you walk.

Fabrics: Make sure the fabric is a type you are willing to take care of. If you've turned your iron into a doorstop, don't buy 100 percent cotton. If you're allergic to your dry cleaner's prices, don't buy wool. Treat your clothes with respect, and they'll give you good service. Prints tend to date a garment quickly; solids stay in fashion longer. Not to say that your closet should be all solids; just be selective and forewarned. Good quality fabric makes any design look better, so buy a few good things. It will save you money in the long run.

These are the things to look for when you shop. What you won't find are many of the amenities our skinny sisters enjoy. A stroll through the misses department of a store reveals mannequins attired in the latest style. Chances are you'll find snappy advertising posters and fancy displays of accessories to assist you in putting together a fashionable new look. Now visit our department, tucked away in the basement next to the clearance center. If you do find a mannequin, it's usually a size ten. I love seeing a size 38 pinned down to fit a size 10 mannequin. Who can tell anything about how a garment will look when the side pockets meet in the back? Fancy accessory displays? Are you kidding? Fat women don't buy accessories or at least that's what most department stores seem to think. Perhaps we haven't bought accessories in the past because we couldn't find them to fit. I doubt that it will break the manufacturers to add a couple of inches to bracelets, belts, and necklaces so we at least have the option to buy or not.

The merchandise in our department may not be as beautifully displayed as it is in the other departments in the store, but that's no reason for us to look as boring as the displays. We've got to learn to be better image shoppers than our tiny sisters if we're going to overcome fatphobia. When I was in college, I worked in a little dress store with a wonderful woman. She told me there's no such thing as an ugly dress. Every dress is waiting for the right body and the right personality to bring it to life. She said, "Some dresses just need a little more attention to bring out their special qualities." We've got to give our clothes a little more attention to bring out their special qualities. In a way, we're lucky. We don't have to settle for prepackaged fashion looks. We can blaze our own fashion trails. Are you ready for the new fashion frontier?

Photo courtesy of YOUNG STUFF a division of Stout Sportswear Group.

Chapter 9

BECOMING A SMART IMAGE SHOPPER

What kind of a shopper are you? Check the phrases that describe you best.

Impulsive Shopper. You need instant gratification. You shop to relieve frustration and tension.

Indecisive Shopper. You can't shop without the opinion of mom, or hubby, or friend. You'll even trust the word of a salesperson working on commission over your own judgment.

Status Shopper. You hope the labels will replace your lack of confidence in your own taste. Unfortunately, price has never been a guarantee of taste.

Stingy Shopper. You demonstrate your self-esteem with your bargain basement clothes. Cheap clothes aren't always a bargain.

Fad Shopper. You hope your outlandish clothes will divert attention from your shortcomings. You'd rather go along with the crowd than think for yourself.

Smart Shopper. You want the best buy at the best price, and you know where to find it.

At times you may be all of these shoppers. We all try to be smart shoppers, but we don't always succeed. I think of smart shoppers as thrifty shoppers. No cheap, not boring, not insecure, just knowledgeable about the products and services we buy. The secret of becoming a smart shopper is working from a plan. Before you can make a plan, you have to inventory your resources. First, tackle your closet. Don't skip this section and go on to the next. Closet cleaning is a vital part of image development. If, after you've read this Section, you still can't face your closet, call a closet cleaning expert.

Bless my home management teacher for showing me that a closet is just an empty space that can be divided according to my needs. I come from a family who used the toss and pile method of closet organization. The T and P method of organization guarantees that whatever you need, it will always be on the bottom and wrinkled.

To organize your closet, you must divide and conquer. Don't skimp on the proper equipment. If the closet has hooks and you like to fold your clothes, buy shelves, instead of hooks. Just about every library has one or two books on closet organization, even if they were published in 1949. Try the **Reader's Guide to Periodical Literature** for more current information. Arm yourself with ideas and examples and attack. Start with two or three hours of free time. The more often you clean your closet, the less time it takes. I tackle my closet two times a year. My house may not get a spring cleaning, but my closet does. After my first closet cleaning session, I went to a local department store and watched a demonstration of space-saving devices. Each year, I put a few new space-savers in my closet. Don't be afraid to toss something out if it doesn't work. Don't devote your life to creating the perfect closet system. My goal is to get the shoes off the floor and find or make a space for everything. It's not terribly scientific, but it works for me.

As you take the clothes out of your closet, begin to sort into three groups. Separate the coordinated outfits into individual pieces. In the first pile will go your favorites, the things you wear all the time and that are in good

Image
Shopper

shape. In the second pile go the garments that need repair, could be updated, or you just can't give up. The third pile will contain the garments you don't wear, don't fit, or are out of date. Group 1, your favorites, go back in the closet arranged according to type—skirts, blouses, dresses, and slacks. Group 3, the rejects, go to Goodwill or a resale shop. As for Group 2, what can be saved? If you just like something, but don't plan to wear it for awhile, put it in a box away from your closet. If it can be altered or repaired, do it before it goes back in the closet. If it's still sitting on your sewing machine after a month, maybe it needs a new home. Now your closet is organized.

You're ready for new closet gadgets that will help keep things neat. Your first investment should be good hangers. I like the oversized plastic ones because they fit the shoulders of my clothes better than wire hangers do. A shoe bag is another must. With a shoe bag, you don't have to get on your hands and knees everytime you need a pair of shoes. Cover the back of your closet door with pegboard, and insert hooks for jewelry, scarves, hats, and belts. A wine rack makes a good place for sweaters. How about a towel rack on the closet door to hang your pants on? You could use hanging baskets for accessories. Cardboard boxes can be covered and stacked in all kinds of ways.

Now you are ready to become an urban guerrilla shopper. Any successful warrior knows you have to have a plan of attack. Start with the magazine pictures you clipped for the visualization exercises. Add other clippings and make an "idea book." Collect pictures of accessories and hairstyles you'd like to try. Don't worry if they're not your size or color, they're just a reminder of what you want to accomplish. Start an information file. Ask questions about where people shop. Find out what kind of free services are available. Many large department stores now have professional image experts who give free advice to customers. They don't care what size you are, as long as you're spending money.

Before you shop, go on a scouting trip. I like to scout alone because I concentrate better and cover more territory. Professional image consultants always scout the market before they meet with a client. Scouting missions are for exploration, not buying. Don't try anything on, just look. Look at fabrics, colors, styles, and prices. Study the display windows and floor mannequins. If you have time, try on a few things you normally wouldn't consider. This kind of experimentation helps you expand your horizons. The object of a scouting trip is to broaden your image potential and find out what's available.

Go back and evaluate your nice, well-organized closet. What should you add to give your wardrobe a fresh, contemporary look? I use color as the basis of my wardrobe plan. I select a dominant shade for expensive items like suits or coats. This dominant shade should be a flattering neutral. Rely on your color analysis to help you select this color. I have a warm/rich skin tone, so I selected brown as my dominant color. If you have a warm/fair skin tone, your best basic color might be warm beige, brown, or light navy. Just about any pink or blue tones would be a good basic color for a cool/fair. For cool/rich skin tones, the dominant colors might be black, white, red, or navy.

As I built my wardrobe, I tried to buy things that would work with this brown group. Just because I wear a lot of brown doesn't mean my wardrobe is boring. I'm careful to include a variety of textures, values, prints, and patterns when I shop. The browns in my wardrobe range from soft tan to rich chocolate. When I got tired of brown, I added a rust group and a forest green group. Occasionally, I'll buy an accent piece that may or may not work with every other group. I try to keep these indulgences inexpensive, so I can add unique points of interest without spending a fortune.

Don't try to improve your whole wardrobe in one shopping trip. Give yourself time to grow in several image directions before you invest too heavily in one look. When I add a color unit, I imagine I'm going away on a weekend trip and I can only take one suitcase. I develop my wardrobe plan from there. Here are some sample wardrobe plans to give you an idea of how to start. This little excursion into your closet is by no means an extensive discussion of wardrobe planning. There are many fine books devoted solely to this topic. Janet Wallach's **Working Wardrobe** is one

Image Shopper

practical guide. Our exercises will get you started. The rest is up to you. If you prefer pants to skirts, substitute them in the basic plan. By now, you know enough about design to alter the wardrobe plan to fit your lifestyle.

Basic Wardrobe Plan—Eight Pieces

I. Tops (Select a total of three.)
Blouses, tops, shirts, lightweight sweaters, etc.

II. Bottoms (Select a total of three.)
Skirts, culottes, pants, shorts, etc.

III. Third Layer (Select one.)
Jackets, cardigans, vests, etc.

IV. Optional (Select one.)
Dress, coat, or additional garment from groups I, II, and III.

Full Wardrobe Plan—Fourteen or More Pieces

I. Tops (Add two.)
II. Bottoms (Add two.)
III. Third Layer (add one or more.)
Optional (Add one or more.)

Compare the clothes you have with your wardrobe plan. The following list may help you see what you need.

Item	Have	Need	Estimated Price
Suits	brown pinstripe	—	—
Skirts	—	brown texture, maybe tweed	$35–$50
Sweaters	beige v-neck	—	—
Blouses	blue silk	off white lace	$25 (?)

Now you try it.

Item	Have	Need	Estimated Price

Scouting the market gives you an idea of how far your budget will stretch. For instance, you'll discover that basic items like velvet blazers come in all price ranges. After closet cleaning, scouting and planning, you'll know what you need, what you can pay, and where you can find it. If there's a limit to your bank account, you may have to learn to wait for the sales. Procrastination can sometimes pay off. It takes nerves of steel to postpone your pleasures but planning a wardrobe is a balancing act. Waiting for the sales takes an act of faith, but most of the time it pays off. With a wardrobe plan, sales can be a real goldmine. Before and after a season are the best time for sales. The trick to buying things on sale is being able to tell whether and how long the item will still be in fashion. Coats are safe sale buys. Since coat styles change slowly, they'll be in fashion for several years to come.

Don't be too quick to judge clothes on a hanger. Some clothes look terrible on the hanger and terrific on you. I was browsing through a sale rack one time when I found a $55 brown knit dress marked down to $13. I almost passed it up because it looked so limp on the hanger. That sale dress looked terrific on me. The hem was the right length for a change and the darts fit perfectly. It looked custom-made. It's still one of my favorites.

Take advantage of the factory outlet stores near you. Every day is sale day there. You'll find seconds, first quality out-of-season merchandise, overstocks, and liquidation stock. You won't find amenities like salespeople and fancy dressing rooms, but if you've got an adventurous spirit the savings are worth it. If you don't have any outlet stores in your town, plan a field trip with some of your friends. It's a good excuse to have fun

Image Shopper

and enjoy their company. Who knows, you might even find a $500 designer coat for $50. It's happened.

To figure out how much I can spend on clothes, I figure how much my husband and I will make in the coming year. Let's say our combined income will be $19,000. After subtracting other anticipated expenses, I'm left with between 5 and 10 percent of our income. I'm feeling optimistic that none of the cars will need major work, so we'll use the 10% figure. Ten percent of $19,000 is $1,900. That means I have $850 dollars to spend on clothes for the year. Now I look at my wish list and find I need a coat, skirt, blouse, pants, and accessories. I shouldn't have any problem finding all these items for well under the $425 I've allotted for my spring and summer wardrobe. When you're first rebuilding your wardrobe, you may not have enough money to do everything in one season or even one year. List your needs in order of importance, and then buy what and when you can. Be flexible enough to take advantage of one-time surprise buys. Once you've budgeted an amount for clothes, try to stick to it. Since I can get carried away with credit cards, I find that shopping with cash helps me stay within my budget. Nothing says you've run out of money better than an empty purse.

To determine if a garment is a bargain, I try to find out it's real cost. I do this by dividing the cost by the number of times I'll wear it. A $50 skirt might seem expensive, until I figure that I'll wear it once every two weeks for two years, or over 52 times. That means the skirt will cost less than a dollar a wearing. If I found a $15 skirt that fell apart after only two wearings, it would cost me $7 a wearing, hardly a bargain.

Are you ready to try your luck? Xerox this list and take it with you when you shop.

1. Do I own anything like it?
2. Do I really need it?
3. Is it the right price?
4. Is this the best time of year to buy it?

5. If it's supposed to be on sale, is it really a bargain?

6. Is there a less expensive item that will work just as well?

7. Are there any disadvantages to this design?

8. Does it really satisfy all my needs?

9. Will the store stand behind its merchandise?

10. How can it be changed to achieve a different look?

11. Does it include a good balance of the elements and principles of design?

12. Does it express my personality and display my personal style?

13. Does it enhance my assets and balance my problems?

14. Is the material good? Is the garment well-made?

15. Can I do the upkeep?

16. Are the applied designs tasteful?

17. Will it be in style for more than a season?

18. Where would it be appropriate to wear?

19. Can I wear it with at least three things I already own?

20. Considering my goals and lifestyle, does it send the right clothing message?

21. Does it fit?

22. What accessories can I use with it to change the mood?

For many of you, the next part will be the hardest. It's easy to fantasize and plan, but it's not always easy to follow through. The true test of your convictions comes when you're at the department store trying to decide between the beautiful but expensive silk, and the nice but ordinary polyester. I found I really had to prepare myself, or else I'd weaken at the last minute and fall back on the old fatphobia stereotypes. During my visualization exercises, I discovered a big part of my desire to be thin was my desire to

Image Shopper

wear certain kinds of clothes that weren't available for fat people. I never questioned the assumption that fat people couldn't wear certain kinds of clothes, and that assumption motivated me to get thin and stay thin. On my first shopping trip I selected one kind of "for skinny only" clothing to try on. I asked myself what kind of clothes made dieting almost worth it. The answer was easy, lacy lingerie. Since I loved it most, it was the last thing I'd allow myself to wear.

I knew I couldn't just go out and buy some sexy lingerie. I'd be so hung up, I wouldn't enjoy the experience. Instead, I started working on visualizing myself, as is, in sexy lingerie. It was hard, and a little funny, at first. But the more I worked on it, the more I really could see myself looking great in certain styles. I gave myself permission to look sexy in pretty lingerie. The first test of my new conviction came when I was shopping with my husband one night. He was looking for a jacket and I was looking for a robe. When Jon didn't find what he wanted, he joined me in looking for a long, safe robe. He turned to a rack of teddies and said, "Why don't you buy one of these? Don't they come in your size?"

I panicked. I wanted to pick a fight, run to the car, do anything but answer his question. Although I'd been working up to buying something sexy, I wasn't ready to put my plan into action. I hoped he was kidding, but before I could think of a good excuse, Jon called a salesperson over. I relaxed a little. I really didn't think they'd have anything in my size. Not only did they have it, it was beautiful—a delicate, dusty rose lace. I wanted it, but I was embarrassed. I almost died when Jon asked me to try it on for him. I almost took it off without letting Jon see me, when I started giggling. What did I care if I shocked a few people? I'd been wanting to break this fatphobia taboo, and now I had my best friend to help me do it. I threw open the curtain and stepped out into the aisle. The two teenaged boys who'd chosen that moment to walk between my husband and the dressing room got an eyeful. It was worth all the embarrassment to see the looks on their faces. All of a sudden, it wasn't scary anymore. I was having a great time. If I hadn't been preparing myself for a change in my image, I probably would have picked a fight with my husband to cover my embarrassment. You can't just change without thinking about it. Prepare yourself and then go for it.

As we wrap up this section on creating a physical image, please allow me a few moments on my soap box. If you don't believe one consumer can make a difference, then you're too young to remember when consumers brought the fashion industry to its knees by refusing to buy midis. They hung on the rack while we continued to wear miniskirts and pantsuits. Consumers have clout, but don't know how or where to use it. We have to educate ourselves, explore our options, and take action.

If we're tired of paying $25 for a pair of jeans that fall apart after one or two washings, we have to speak up. If we sit around quietly, the fashion industry will think we're satisfied with shoddy, overpriced merchandise. If the stores get a few customers armed with sales receipts and angry words, they'll stop buying clothes from those manufacturers. The stores would rather switch than fight. Part of the reason designers and retailers haven't known what we wanted is that we haven't been able to speak their language. After reading Chapter 8, you can tell them you want unique, quality clothes, clothes for fat women. If we don't speak, they'll never hear us.

You've got to let your voice be heard at least once. Imagine what would happen if all 20 million fat women in this country spoke up. I know it takes time and effort, but that's the only way for us to be taken seriously. Select one thing that really makes you mad. Maybe you're tired of tops that are too short for tall people. Maybe you're tired of never finding youthful styles for big women. Maybe you're tired of everything being made of polyester. Maybe you'd like to see some high fashion for big women. Maybe you're tired of the makeup department not taking you seriously when you want to sample something new. Once you get started, you may not want to stop, especially if your complaint is acted on.

Don't complain to the salesperson or the department manager, find out who the person in charge is. Complain directly to the designer or the manufacturer about a product. Go to the head of the company to complain about a service. Don't be intimidated; these people want to hear what their customers think. Complaining in person is most effective, but takes guts. Registering your complaint in writing is the next best thing, and it's not as scary. Tell them in calm, precise language what they've done to displease you. Don't swear or start ranting. One letter of complaint I wrote to a grocery store president brought a lawyer and the district manager to my door with apologies. Another letter ended up in the editorial page of the newspaper. People will listen if you speak up.

Organize your friends. One letter might make a businessman stop and think. Six letters will throw him into a panic. The more the owner sees the need (profit potential), the more interested he or she becomes. Carole Shaw, editor of **Big Beautiful Woman** magazine, publishes "Mad as Hell" coupons in each issue. You xerox these coupons and send one to the offending company and one to her magazine, so they have a record of the complaint. The company may toss your coupon in the wastebasket, but Carole won't forget them. By going on record with your complaint you'll be helping all of us.

Now that we have a clearer picture of what we want, we don't have to limit ourselves to ready-to-wear clothes. With our new image-building system, we can design our own clothes. I'm aware some people don't like to sew. A fashion editor once confided that her first sewing project made her break out in hives. It is possible to have the variety, fit, and fun of custom-made clothes without having to sew a stitch. Custom-made clothes are affordable. Have you priced good ready-to-wear clothes lately? Let's compare. If you find a ready-to-wear suit in the $150 to $175 price range, a similar custom-made suit might require notions and five yards of wool, $12 to $15 a yard—a total of $75 to $90. The seamstress will probably charge between $50 and $75 for her work. Both suits cost about the same, but the custom-made suit has given the added satisfaction of helping to design it.

Most fabric stores and department stores that sell fabric have a list of local seamstresses. Some fabric stores even have added a wardrobe planning service. If you don't have any luck, call a local college with a home economics or fashion design department. Most students would love to pick up extra money by using their sewing skills. Some seamstresses advertise in the newspaper under personal services or in the yellow pages under women's apparel. Don't forget to ask the people you meet if they know someone who sews for a living. Call around to find out what the going rates are. Most seamstresses charge by the hour or by the garment. Plan on paying a fair hourly rate. I'd pay a seamstress $5 an hour now, since the minimum wage is about $3.50 an hour. Seamstresses who charge more than this should be really exceptional. Tailoring costs more because it takes more time and skill. In the San Francisco area, I'd expect to pay a seamstress $15 to $25 for a skirt or blouse, and anywhere between $25 and $50 for dress or jacket that didn't require tailoring.

Interview your potential seamstress in person. Ask about her experience and check her references. Ask to see samples of her work. If you're satisfied put the price and due date in writing. A deposit may be required, but don't pay in full until the work has been completed to your satisfaction. If you exercise the same care in selecting a seamstress that you do in shopping, you shouldn't have any problems. You may want your seamstress to come along on your first few trips to the fabric store, especially if you don't sew yourself. That way you'll be sure she can make the garment you want. Make sure she's experienced enough to handle basic alterations, like changing sleeve styles or leg widths. Having your seamstress with you will guarantee you select the right fabric for your design.

I hope this idea will encourage large women who sew to go into business for themselves. Good clothes are so expensive that a good, reasonably-priced seamstress could make money and satisfy her customer's desire for well-made clothes at the same time. If you've been toying with the idea of going into business, this may be a way to start. If you don't sew, consider opening a large size resale shop. Most regular resale shops aren't interested in large sizes, so if you've got the cash and the talent—a boutique that takes large size designs on consignment would be a great idea. We can change what's going on in the fashion world if we get off our ample fannies

Image Shopper

148

and do it. When I see all the talent around me, I'm certain we can work together to better our lot.

You're about to graduate. Now you know how images are developed, so here's your final exam.

1. Is your new image in keeping with current fashion trends, your age, occupation, and environment?
2. Does your new image meet your standards of taste? Is it appropriate?
3. Are you paying attention to details such as fingernails, makeup, and hair?
4. Are you learning how to get others to assist you in your image development?
5. Are you taking time to grow into your new image?
6. Are you more careful when you shop? Do you look for fit and quality?
7. Are you making an effort to express all facets of your lifestyle in the way you dress?
8. Are you beginning to like yourself better?
9. Are you beginning to value the unique contributions you have to make?
10. Are you trying to balance the **yin** and **yang** aspects of your physical and mental self?
11. Are you paying close attention to the colors you wear?
12. Do your actions fit your image?
13. Are you exploring ways to improve your posture, voice, and nonverbal communication?
14. Are you taking better care of your body, no matter what your size?
15. Are you working on your visualization exercises?

If you answered yes to most of these questions, then you're on the road to freedom from fatphobia. Face the poster of our patron saint, Miss Piggy, and repeat after me:

I Promise:

- Never to wear clothes more than five years out of date.
- Never to wear clothes that don't fit.
- Never to buy any more unbecoming clothes.
- Never to buy on impulse again.
- Never to wear dirty clothes or clothes in need of repair.
- Never to rely on fatphobia stereotypes to guide my selection of clothes.

I Promise:

- To enhance my assets **now.**
- To emphasize what is important in each life situation when it comes to clothes.
- To keep my clothing goals in mind when I shop.
- To concentrate on building my image everyday.
- To appreciate and accept what God has given me, and do my best to realize my potential.

Image Shopper

Photo courtesy of Lane Bryant.

Chapter 10

SOUNDS GOOD SO FAR, BUT DOES IT WORK?

You've taken your time, energy, and resources to develop your image. Now, you're wondering if it will really help. Can the deep-rooted prejudices against fat be changed? Is looking like everyone else going to be enough? I wondered the same thing, so I interviewed people to see if other big women have come to terms with their bodies and with society's attitudes about them. Much to my surprise, I found many success stories. Some had been large all their lives, some had not. Some had found self-acceptance through therapy, Overeaters Anonymous, or private counseling groups.

Amid the painful experiences, there were many shining success stories. These woman gave me hope. If a few special women could overcome fat-phobia, isolated as they were in their struggle, our collective strength would make the process easier. The stories that follow are examples of the people who gave me courage to write this book.

Anita Ohearn (with microphone) and model Clemintina Depae

Anita Ohearn:
Bigger Than Life
Owner, Anita Ohearn Productions
Lafayette, California

In the early days of my modeling career, I answered an ad in the local paper for large size models. I found more than a job, I found a friend. Anita Ohearn is the embodiment of all the magical characters that she portrays. At Christmas, you'll find her at the local mall as Mrs. Santa Claus. At Halloween, she's the Big Pumpkin. At Easter, she's Esther Bunny. All fourteen of her characters sparkle with Anita's warm personality.

"After years of thinking my weight was responsible for my lack of success, I finally had some counseling. I found out the weight had nothing to do with my lack of success. In fact, I discovered it actually helped me, since I play larger-than-life characters. It also helps me when I present a fashion clinic for large women, because I've been there.

"For years I didn't feel I could be beautiful. But, I think attitudes are changing now. I used to get more negative feedback. Now I have strangers walk up to me and tell me how beautiful I am. Ninety percent of it is self-image.

I'd wish I'd learned that sooner. Be happy within yourself. Be up front about what you want."

Anita has come a long way from that little girl nicknamed "Frog." One of the major stresses in her life was her relationship with men.

"Junior high was tough. I was so much bigger than the other kids that I felt like I had to be careful not to hurt them. I think I dated two boys in high school. Although I hated cliques, I was part of the upper crust. I was an honor student, a kind of a maverick sharpie. My emerging, funny personality helped me get by.

"I was always so big and tall that I had to work on being feminine. I used to worry about how men would feel about me when I was thin. A lot of large ladies are scared of the sexual connotations of being thin. I'm still working on this dilemma.

"I've been on diets—starvation diets. My life was dominated by dieting. I felt like I'd lost control of my life. I don't respond well to negative reinforcement. A slap on the hand when I gain a pound doesn't work. Telling me I'm a bad girl just makes me into a binge. Give me strokes, positive reinforcement, and then I respond."

Anita recently switched from teaching handicapped children to running a full time production company. "I teach voice lessons and have fashion clinics. Then I play my characters. I just held a Fantasy Day at a local school. I dress up as one of my characters and teach a special lesson in art, music, or drama. Putting on a costume changes attitudes about my size. That makes me both happy and sad. Some people think those of us who are overweight lack character and willpower. It's not true. It's sad that some people have to see me in costume to see me as a person. Never judge a person by the amount of space they occupy—mental or body space. That goes for knocking small people if you're big. It's bad enough that it's happened to us. Let's not become size bigots ourselves.

Remember that success is in the mind of the person trying to be successful. Use symbols and visualization exercises. And play up your feminity. We have seen a lot of anger emerge from the discussion of bigness. I went through a time when I was angry too. But now I want to see big women as the great masters saw them—elegant and feminine.

Diane Worthington

Diane Worthington:
A Great Big Success
Owner, Zoftig San Francisco, California

I was in San Francisco covering the opening of the first high fashion boutique exclusively for large women when I met Diane Worthington. The opening was an exquisite affair. We drank champagne out of crystal glasses and ate very expensive chocolates. The last taboo had been broken. Now large women can have it all—from French pastries to French cut lingerie. The food was almost as delicious as the clothes. Thanks to Diane, large women now had the option of designer clothes.

Sophisticated energetic Diane is the classic big woman. With the exception of a few bouts of dieting, she has always been large. "I've always been big. My grandmother, mother, and sister are big. In sixth grade I weighed 188 pounds. I hated being weighed in gym class. I'd try to cover the scale so my classmates wouldn't tease me to death. I tried dieting, but it never worked because I thought I didn't have any willpower. I don't feel out of control now, but I sure did back then. I tried all the teenage diets.

"In high school, I remember feeling relieved because being big seemed to put me out of the competition. I felt above it all, but on another level, I still wanted success with boys. I think it allowed me to have more female friendships because I wasn't competing.

I had the usual fat girl problems. I dated boys, but they got teased about it. I found myself helping them hide the fact we were dating.

"When I was fifteen, my mother decided I should have a career, so she sent me to beauty school. It wasn't for me. I never learned to type because I didn't want to end up being a secretary. I wanted to use my creativity.

"My attitude about myself changed when I was about twenty. I wanted to see the world, so I traveled to Europe, Canada, Mexico, Asia and Africa. I even landed in Paris during the 1968 riots. That's when I found out big women are appreciated in some countries. I was pinched in Italy. I had a Pakistani propose to me in Afghanistan. We were having dinner one night and he turned to me and said "Diane, you are so . . . fat." My friends at the table had to laugh because they knew in his country he was giving me the ultimate compliment. At first it made me uncomfortable to be wanted because I was fat. I felt weight shouldn't be an issue one way or the other. I didn't want men to love me just for my body. I've tried not to be affected by the flack society gave me about being large or being a woman. Being fat is a problem only if you let it be one.

"I was involved with a concert promotion company in Canada. I was responsible for travel arrangements, advertising, and bookings. I handled some big stars. I found there was a lot of discrimination against women in the music business. I put on some good shows to let people know I could do a good job. The hard work almost killed me.

Eventually I moved back to the United States and started a mail order business. I designed, manufactured, and marketed my own line of large size clothes. I'd included a questionaire with each order, and I got them back by the thousands. That's when I realized that so many women shared the same problems in finding decent clothes. That's when I got the idea for Zoftig. I wanted to create a comfortable environment.

"We've been open for five months now and I'm delighted at how well we're doing. We've doubled our inventory since we opened. If things go well here I'd like to open branches in other major cities. We'd like to start support groups too.

"To me, service is everything. Our customers like the store and they want us to succeed. We know all our customers by name. We do whatever we can to improve the self-images of the women who come in. "Customers know we're honest. If something doesn't look good, we'll tell them. Because of this, they're willing to try new things.

"I was a panelist on a talk show recently. The subject was discrimination against large women. I told the host, 'Of course large people are going to be depressed if all they have to wear is black polyester. That's enough to depress you.' The image you project determines how people will treat you. If you look dowdy, you won't get the treatment you deserve. But if you look like a million bucks, you'll get the respect and consideration you deserve.

"When I went on an unsuccessful diet in 1977, I found I was the same person, fat or thin. I still had the same complex life issues to work through. Large women should learn to follow their hearts and not the feedback and interference they get from society. Don't be afraid of being large. Do what you want to do. When you're making a decision you know is right, follow your heart."

Jeri Harris: It's Tough Being in the Middle
Manager, Yardage Fair Pleasant Hill, California

Jeri and I have known each other since we were both salesclerks at the store she now manages. In those days, she was big, tall, happy, and self-confident. I always admired Jeri because, while I was killing myself with diets, she exuded confidence. Jeri represents another kind of big woman. She's in the middle—not small, but not classicially large. After losing sixteen pounds, she has gone from a "tight 16 to a loose 14." Being in the middle can be the most frustrating, because you tend to feel almost normal. Believing you need to lose five pounds can create as much stress as feeling you have to lose fifty.

Jerri Harris

"I've accepted the fact that I'm not going to be small. Now I dress for it. I can show my figure off. I can be attractive and be large. I think having others say big is okay has helped me accept myself. Clothes are changing in the stores and even in the pattern books.

"I lost the weight mainly for my health. My father died of a heart attack, and I inherited his small veins. I'd still like to lose a few pounds, but I accept myself now. Actually, my weight loss was due to a combination of things. My husband was getting too chunky so I put him on a diet. We just started eating sensibly. We don't cheat ourselves, we're just more conservative. Instead of eating a whole cake by ourselves, I bring it to work. I've gotten into exercise, too. I used to think I got enough exercise working here. Now I do it because it makes me feel good. I like it. Another thing is I'm happy with my life. I like my job. The growth in the store makes me feel good. My husband is through school, and he finally has a job.

"I still have to watch myself, especially when I'm bored. If I don't want to sew, on my days off, I find others things to keep me from slipping back. I'll take a walk. I've learned to tune into hunger and what I eat. I don't know that it was a conscious change. I don't tell myself 'you're going to have a carrot.' I just started doing it. My husband says you know you are really hungry when you want meat or cheese instead of a cookie.

"I used to eat when I was happy, or sad, or nervous, especially in high school. I wouldn't even think about what I ate—it was just a diversion. I used it so I wouldn't have to face certain problems. I'd eat everything to try to justify. When I got married, it seemed okay to eat because I was married and I didn't have to compete anymore. On my last diet, I lost weight and then started eating because I felt I deserved to. Because I lost the weight. I'd start thinking of excuses to celebrate so I could eat.

"I started gaining weight when I was eleven. My father died and I got my first bra—a lot of things were changing. All of a sudden I started getting heavy, but I don't remember changing my eating habits. My teen years were extremely rough. I didn't date. After I finished school, I went wild. My weight fluctuated a lot. I was at a good weight when I married my husband. He's always supported me and thought I was attractive. It was me who didn't. Only after a few men flirted with me did I begin to believe that maybe I did look okay.

Now I've learned you have to accept yourself for what you are. Don't try to be someone else. You can be feminine and large at the same time. I can have a job with responsibility and I can still be feminine."

I asked Jeri what would happen if she gained the weight back. How would it affect her self-esteem?

"If I gained it back, I'd like to say it wouldn't matter, but I think I'd be a little unhappy with myself. I'd be unhappy because I'd feel I had failed. I'm eating good, I'm not depriving myself. If I put the weight back on, it would be because I'm shoving food in my mouth for emotional reasons, and that would make me unhappy."

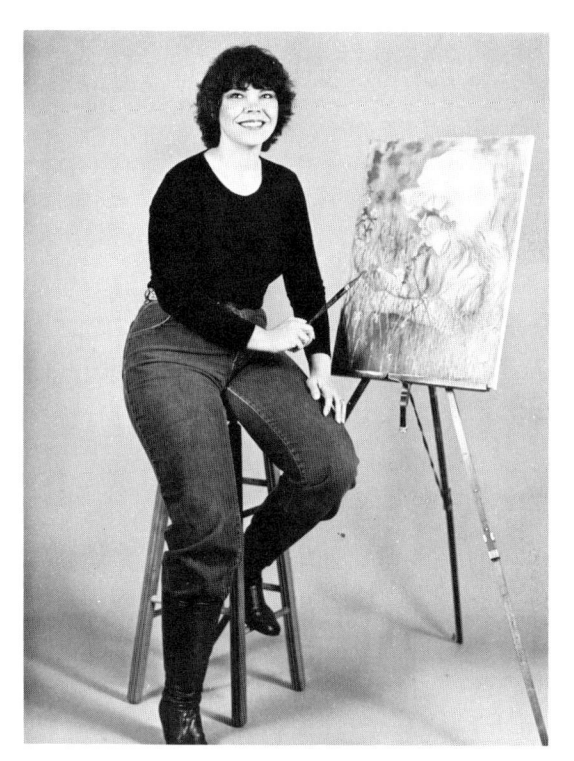

Christina Urbanik

Christina Urbanik: All I Wanted Was a Pair of Size 14 Jeans
Counselor Pleasanton, California

I met Chris in one of the groups that I interviewed. Her strong sense of self that emerged after years of struggling against body size prejudice is noteworthy. For her, being large has meant living with the stereotype of the over-endowed sex symbol.

"I started going to dances when I was twelve. I enjoyed an active social life. Older men liked me. They paid attention to me. They'd say I was pretty, or sweet, or cute. I didn't get involved with older men, but the boys I dated were older.

"When I was fourteen we moved to South Carolina, and I gained a lot of weight. I began to eat out of frustration. I was a bright person, but we were poor. I didn't have any challenges, so I ate. I used my body to get attention and affection. I had no respect for myself. Throughout my teens, I was always bigger than other girls. I tried to fit in by wearing the same styles my petite friends did. I tried to fit my personality to that standard. It wasn't until I got older that I realized I had a nice body. "When I was twelve, I lived with my mother and my sister. Neither of them had very much self-esteem. I saw how they threw themselves at men. It was terrible to see the way men treat women. Because of those experiences, I became terrified of men. Only when I taught classes mostly made up of men did I come to terms with my fear.

"There were three things that helped me come to terms with my weight: going to work with a lot of men, a national support group, and my cousin. The support group helped a lot. My cousin, who is two years older, helped me a lot. She overcame her compulsive eating problem at an early age. She helped by giving me support and encouragement. She helped my self-esteem. Those three things, along with writing and looking at the phases of my life, helped me overcome my problem.

"It has taken three years of hard work to see myself as a person of value. It really started to change about a year ago. At one time, my biggest goal was to wear a pair of size 14 jeans. Now, I have three pairs. When I have my bad days now, I think that's not good enough. I used to think all I wanted was to be thin. Now the most important thing is to stop my compulsive eating. I don't want food to be the center of my life. I want to be healthy and pretty. Now I can think. Now I can function.

"I've learned that eating won't make me feel better about myself. Everyone has bad days. I know I'm more than a body. For the most part, I feel good about myself. But when I am feeling bad, I focus on where the problems are coming from. It may have nothing to do with food.

"Compulsive eating is my problem. There were times when I wanted to die because I couldn't quit eating. I couldn't live with the pain. It controlled my life. Now, I'm not afraid to look at who I really am. When you're willing to take an honest look at yourself, you'll find the things you were scared of don't exist. Don't be afraid to go to any lengths to find the beautiful person within you.

"The most important advice I want to share with other big women concerns men. I lot of women don't like themselves because they've dealt with men who'd criticize you, no matter what your size. They'd never see your beauty because they're too busy looking at themselves. It wouldn't matter to them if you were perfect, they'd still hurt you. These are the Prince Charmings of the world—only charming until you get to know them. Look to the frogs instead. Inside them you'll find princes. These are the men who'll support you, love you, and help you find the beautiful woman inside."

Sandra Hunnicutt: The Change Has Begun
Public Health Nurse and Teacher San Jose, California

Modeling is only one of Sandi's many talents. Our paths crossed at a large size fashion show when I was the commentator and she was one of the models. After the show, we walked about consciousness-raising and the big woman. She told me she'd been teaching self-esteem classes for seven years.

"When I first started teaching these classes, I took a pretty routine approach. I felt that once you lost the weight, you'd become acceptable and everything would fall in place. A lot of things happened in my personal life that helped change my approach. I sought counseling because I was going crazy in my marriage. My husband had convinced me that I did everything to compensate for the fact that I was fat. My counselor helped me see that

I'd lost my identity in that relationship. I went home and asked for a divorce.

"I spent over a year on my own, trying to find out who I was. I found a man who could accept me for who I was, even at 240 pounds. I also got involved in the holistic health movement. About the same time I found **Fat Is a Feminist Issue.** It gave me permission to stop trying to please everybody. In September 1979, I started teaching 'Fat is Not About Food.' I lost forty-five pounds in six months, and I've kept it off without dieting. I've found it's an on-going process. I still gain during a major crisis, such as my father's death."

Sandra Hunnicutt

Sandi's life seems to fit a classic pattern. "Childhood was very painful. I remember hearing my mother's friends whispering about my baby fat. When I was eleven they said my period would make the fat go away. It didn't happen. Then it was supposed to go away when I got married. It didn't happen. Then it was supposed to get better if I got pregnant. It didn't. When I got a divorce, it got better.

"I remember my parents arguing over me. I expected my father to defend me, but he never did. I became an overachiever in high school to compensate for not dating. I was a leader. I could organize other people. I did go to the prom. I had a nice dress, and I looked nice. I kept wondering what the problem was. Why wasn't I asked to dance? All I could figure out was it was because I was fat."

Sandi now teaches others how to overcome their problems. "Success means people leave the course with a vibrant attitude about themselves, their relationships, and their bodies. They're no longer focused on food, fads, and fat. They emerge encouraged and excited about who they are and what they have to offer. Weight loss, if it occurs, is a by-product of self-acceptance.

"My advice is: learn to accept who you are, and stop blaming your successes and failures on how you look. We are each a gift to each other. I have something to give you, and you have something to give to me. The exchange won't take place if you're preoccupied with comparing your body to someone else's. We have to learn to accept people's differences. If we can't get along with ourselves, how will we be able to get along with others? If we get bogged down by stereotypes, humanity suffers a great loss."

Photo courtesy of Lane Bryant.

Chapter 11

INSTEAD OF AN EATING PROGRAM, TRY A PEOPLE PROGRAM

It seems we've spent most of the book talking about physical image. Actually, we've done a great deal of work on the inner person at the same time. You can't change one without affecting the other. We must continue the changes we've begun. One way to do this is to form a support group. It can give you a safe environment in which to get feedback on your growth process. I've spoken to you as an expert, now I'm speaking as a friend who's shared your experience. It's been hard to compress two decades of searching into a few hundred pages. I was afraid I'd forget some vital element that would be the key to overcoming fatphobia. Then I realized I didn't have to spoon-feed every morsel of information to you. A 1980 survey by **Big, Beautiful Woman** magazine indicated 70 percent of its readers were high school graduates and one-third had completed college. You know how to research and analyze. All you need is a little help finding the right direction. You can handle it from there.

As a matter of fact, you probably want to take an active part in your own education. If you're like me, you're tired of people who try to force information down your throat, as if you couldn't think for yourself. Get involved in your education so it will leave a lasting impression. Education that doesn't change a person's life is useless. If you accept someone else's version of the truth without question, you'll end up questioning yourself. Question attitudes and authority. What kind of advice are they giving you about fat, body size, self-image, self-worth, and nutrition? Asking questions is essential to your growth.

I'm not a crusader by nature. I hated to admit I'm fat, much less reveal the crazy things I've done in the name of dieting. When I finally discovered that fatphobia was the cause of the years of pain, isolation, and self-hatred. I realized it was my responsibility to pass on the wisdom that freed me. As long as I was making fighting fat my avocation, I might as well help others in their struggle.

Now you have to rise to the challenge. Leave the safe, predictable world of dieting and face the truth about fat. But don't make your struggle a solitary one. My task is almost complete, but yours is just beginning. I envy you, because the journey is as important as the destination. A whole new world of confidence and self-respect awaits you. During those years I struggled with my weight, I knew the answer had to be right in front of me, but I couldn't see it. I felt if I were good enough, I'd be rewarded with a simple solution. When I finally started piecing the puzzle together, I realized that the process of discovering fatphobia was much like feminist consciousness-raising.

Consciousness-raising changed my life. But in battling fatphobia, I needed the kind of support the consciousness-raising model avoids. I knew the group setting was the perfect answer, but we needed to do more than just raise our level of awareness. So I began to search for the kind of group techniques that would best serve my purpose.

I decided that overcoming fatphobia doesn't require a therapy group. Therapy can sometimes be overly problem-oriented, and our fatphobia group needs to deal with people, not just their problems. The group won't solve our problems, it will, instead, be a place to work on our development. Sensitivity training and encounter groups have their place, but we shouldn't rely on confrontational techniques. We are looking for the honesty these kinds of groups encourage, but we don't need to drag the truth out of people.

We don't want a bitch session or a coffeeklatch. These kinds of groups can be great for letting off steam, but we need to direct our energies, not just find a release for them. We need to turn our anger outward to understand and fight fatphobia. A support group can be helpful in overcoming fatphobia because it gives people a place to verbalize. We don't need amateur shrinks giving advice that may work for them but not for the person with the problem.

We need to learn the problem-solving techniques that allow us to explore solutions in a supportive atmosphere. We need to have lesson plans, assignments, and a teacher to help guide our growth. What we need is a combination of class, consciousness-raising group, and support group. What will we call it? How about Fatphobia Awareness Training, or FAT, for short? The title tells the world we're gathering together to explore the implications of being fat in a world obsessed with being thin. You may object to belonging to a FAT Group at first, but as you explore compulsive eating and the other aspects of being fat, you'll see how important it is to confronting the issue directly.

I tried some of my new techniques on some of the women I interviewed for **Big & Beautiful**, and they worked. We left each group stronger, more aware, and feeling better about ourselves. But I still wasn't convinced. Then I discovered that Sandi Hunnicutt, the teacher you met in Chapter

10, had been using similar techniques with great success. Sandi has been teaching her body size awareness class for seven years. She allowed me to interview the women in one of her classes. The results of her techniques were amazing. The women had achieved a great deal of insight into the problems caused by fatphobia. Because of Sandi's class, they were better prepared to handle fatphobia stereotypes.

It's easy to see from their comments how much Sandi's class has meant to these women.

> **Joyce:** I thought I was the only compulsive eater in the world. My mother made me so ashamed that I had to lie and sneak food. I couldn't believe other people believed and acted as I did. I thought I was the only one. I thought everyone else who was fat was fat because they had medical problems."
>
> **Alice:** "Today I care about myself. When I walk into a room, people know that I care about myself. I always used to hate myself and my body. Today I don't."
>
> **Pam:** "Taking this class has improved my sex life because I've discovered that I'm a sexy, sensual person. The other night, I put on a nightgown I'd had just for our wedding night, and my husband went crazy. So now I've been putting on really nice gowns at night."
>
> **Ann:** "I've gotten in touch with my assertiveness. It's important to stay in touch with who you are, how you view yourself, and what your limits are. In other words, say no with your mouth instead of your fat."
>
> **Patti:** "One of the things I've learned is that I can make a conscious choice in my life. I made a conscious choice that I didn't want to weigh 210 pounds. I was miserable there for many reasons. I don't know all of them yet, but I'm working on it. If I make the choice that this is where I want to stay then I'll accept myself and be happy."

Sandi's success, along with the increasing number of similar classes, convinced me my technique would work.

Sandra Hunnicutt, teacher of body size acceptance classes in San Jose, California and her students. Group involvement and discussion boosts self-confidence and image. From left to right: students, Barbara Seifert, Ervinette Dilger, Beverly Foster

My actual group experience is limited compared to the dozens of similar groups and classes have popped up in the last two years. Each one uses slightly different techniques and terms, but the result is the same. Some of the programs still stress being thin as the ultimate goal but most are helping people learn to accept themselves as they are. If you want to be thin, that's fine. But there is an alternative to the traditional dieting regime.

Why does the group experience work in overcoming fatphobia? Fatphobia is a complex problem. Diets and other techniques focus on the symptoms, rather than the overall patterns of behavior. Fatphobia needs to be analyzed on both the conscious and unconscious levels. In a group each member can draw on a variety of ideas, options, and experiences in dealing with their problems. The sum total of the group's experiences provides a wide base for defining the problem and finding solutions to it. Each individual's experiences help create part of the solution.

Many people believe they can never be thin enough, and, as a consequence they fear fat. Their fears tend to isolate fat people. Eating becomes a solitary act like masturbation. Isolation can cause physical and emotional problems. Sharing your feelings and experiences with a group brings you an enormous sense of relief. You find you're not alone. But only when you find the courage to admit fatphobia affects you, will you meet your fellow sufferers. Take heart for you are not a freak, nor are you a failure.

The group discussions will help you see you're fat for good reasons. We're fat because we use food to cope with situations we can't deal with in other ways. The group can help you understand the origins and purpose of, and find a solution to, your compulsive eating problem. If you deal only with your symptoms, the underlying problem usually manifests itself in other, equally negative, ways. A person who starts smoking to deal with the anxiety caused by the diet is an example of this. With the support of a group you are more likely to discover the reasons for the behavior. Knowing why you do something is the first step in the process of change. As you see others controlling their compulsive eating, you'll find ways to control your problem. The group can provide support and comfort for the times when you can't seem to get food out of the center of your life. You'll learn that allowing yourself to be fat and happy doesn't mean you've given up.

Everyone is afraid of rejection. Many of us postpone living, isolating ourselves at home, because we're afraid we'll be rejected for being fat. We spend our lives trying to compensate for an imagined flaw that our fear of rejection magnifies a hundredfold. The feedback you get from the group will help you get a realistic perspective of your life and your problems. You can practice being normal in a safe, friendly environment. The support you'll receive will help reaffirm your feelings of self-worth. In a FAT group, you'll begin to see that fat is just an adjective. Fat will lose its ability to hurt you. You can practice dealing with the subtle and not-so-subtle discrimination you experience as a fat person. In the group, you'll help expose the sources of that discrimination. The group experience works because fatphobia prejudice like all prejudice, is based on opinion, not fact. Opinions **can** be changed. A FAT group will help you effect that

People Program

change in yourself and in others. FAT Groups won't dictate your thinking, they'll just help direct your education.

Until we learn to trust our instincts, we'll never be happy. The more you're true to yourself, the easier it is to meet your needs. The goal of every group member is to conquer the addiction to food. Compulsive eating is the major symptom of this addiction. We need to regain our self-confidence and self-respect. This doesn't necessarily mean we have to lose weight. Having a smaller body doesn't uncover the reasons you're a compulsive eater. Only when we've accomplished all of the following, will we have overcome fatphobia:

- Understand the symbolic meanings of fat and thin.
- Learn new ways to deal with hunger.
- Understand you are not alone in your struggle.
- Learn how compulsive eating makes you powerless.
- Understand why fatphobia exists.

The First Meeting

So you can get a better idea of what a group experience might be like, I've combined several groups to create a fairly typical sample group. The names are invented. Pretend it's 7:30 p.m—time for our first FAT group meeting. As you approach the meeting place, you can feel the butterflies in your stomach. The woman whose ad you answered seemed nice enough on the phone, but you're still scared. The door opens, revealing women of varying body sizes. Some are talking in small groups, others are quietly watching.

The leader opens the meeting by asking everyone to introduce herself. After the introductions, Carla, the group leader, tells her fat story. To help each member understand what brought her to a FAT group, everyone is encouraged to share her experiences. All the laughter and sharing make 10 p.m. arrive too soon. Plans are made for the next meeting, lessons are handed out, and arrangements for refreshments are made. A roomful of strangers have become friends. In the week that follows, friendships blossom within the group. Several members plan to walk together for pleasure. By the next meeting, twelve of the original fifteen members gather to resume their work.

The Second Meeting

This week Carla begins the meeting by encouraging each member to relate one good thing that happened during the last week. At first, the experiences shared are minor, insignificant and impersonal, but Carla knows it takes time for each new group to build the trust that fosters personal disclosure. Carla then reads a lesson to the group. Each lesson is a summary of the research done by the group or the group leader. This lesson deals with the process of changing our attitudes.

"How do we change ourselves so that we can change the world? Some call it behavior modification, others call it problem-solving. I like to call it attitude redirection. Whatever you call it, the conclusion is the same: if you love the habit more than you want the cure, you'll never get rid of the habit. Nature abhors a vacuum. If you break a habit and don't find another outlet for that energy, you'll go back to the habit. To change your behavior for good, you have to fill the vacuum. Redirecting your attitude will help you focus on the positive, rather than the negative, aspects of your life. The more you move in a new direction, the less you'll miss the old habit.

"Most of us prefer easy solutions to our problems. Wouldn't it be nice if we were each issued a magic wand, and with one wave all our problems would be solved. Since this isn't likely to happen, we'll have to settle for changing our thinking. All you have to do is just point your mind in the right direction and your troubles will be over. Sounds too easy, doesn't it? We know nothing is ever as easy as it sounds. There are risks involved in making changes. Considering the risk is good because it reduces your chances of failure, but being terrified of taking risks is bad. Don't worry so much about risk-taking that you never accomplish anything. Once you've decided change, your momentum will keep moving you forward. Every step forward you take lessens the risk involved.

"Attitude redirection isn't a smooth, streamlined process. You'll experience many emotions as you embark on your journey. You may be overwhelmed by the amount of information on the subject of fat. An overdose of information can cause paralysis, so be careful not to overdo.

If you do overdose, step back from the problem for a while. "During the search this FAT group will help you with, you may experience anger, denial, guilt, depression, and finally acceptance. All these emotions are an important part of your growth, so don't despair. The most difficult obstacle may be learning how to be selective about which options you apply to your life. Your campaign against fatphobia will be different from everyone else's. The constant questioning that goes on in this group may make you uneasy at times, but it is essential that you develop a certain degree of skepticism, especially where advice from strangers is concerned. Attitude redirection means thinking for yourself. It requires you to

- realize you have choices;
- question the status quo;
- make a commitment, because success is achieved by inches; and
- take action, because the best ideas don't help anyone if you keep them in your head."

Carla now encourages everyone to discuss and sort out the information presented in the lesson. She asks questions that will provoke analysis. The group members will uncover new information from their own experiences. The object of Carla's questioning is not to arrive at an answer, but to explore avenues of future study.

After the lesson, our group discussed where we get our attitudes about proper body size.

Sandy: "I think a lot of it has to do with advertising. Every magazine has the latest fad diet. All the clothes these days are made for slim figures. I think the whole belief system is bad, starting with **Seventeen** magazine, no, even before that. It sets a woman up to believe that she has to look a certain way and if she doesn't look a certain way, then she's a mess as a woman."

Kay: "And the woman's magazines—wow. You'd think this would be a perfect opportunity for magazines like **Working Woman** to change the way these women look. I want t see a woman on the cover who has some real character—not just a flashy businesswoman."

Debbie: "Personally, I don't want to be overweight. I feel better about myself if I'm not overweight. Maybe it's because of magazines and advertising, and what men think. What ever those reasons are, that's alright. I succumb to them."

Carla then leads the group in the discussion of possible solutions, from which each individual member will create her own plan of attack. Use games and exercises as tools to aid your exploration, and to make the experience more interesting and fun. Carla's group discussed these options:

Jane: "We've got to stop assuming fat is a symptom of an emotional or personal problem. We've got to stop blaming ourselves. We can fight back, even if it's just with words."

Sandy: "The problem is fat people think fat is bad. We are always qualifying ourselves because of our condition. Every time you see a movie star on TV, they are always talking about having to lose weight, especially the fat ones. It's as if they are using dieting as an excuse to be accepted as normal."

Barbara: "The National Association to Aid Fat Americans doesn't believe you have to be thin to deserve to be human. They consider it bad taste to comment negatively about another person's appearance. I read that in an article. I think that's good. Thin shouldn't be a condition required to be part of the human race. Maybe we should write to them for more information."

Edna: "Well, I'm going to stop making a career out of being fat. I'm tired of feeling defensive, guilty, and embarrassed all the time. I think if we do regain our perspective and get a better sense of humor, it will help. I've got more important things to worry about. My kids are enough to drive anyone crazy without worrying about my dress size."

Their discussion about how to change people's attitudes reminded me of the first time I was interviewed as a spokeswoman for the rights of fat people. I tried to emphasize the positive aspects of being big, and how great I thought a new view of fat people would be for everyone. The reporter kept wanting to discuss the negative aspects of being fat. I refused to dwell on the pain and discrimination fat people experience. After a few more minutes, the reporter closed her notebook and said, "If nothing bad has happened to you as the result of being fat, I don't see any story. Besides, you look normal to me." That made me mad, but I didn't want to blow it? Why did she want me to rehash the problems? I wanted to spread the good news that things were changing.

I went into the interview thinking I could change her attitudes by emphasizing the positive. I realized I had to change my strategy if I was going to salvage the interview. She didn't see a story, so I had to show her that one existed. I wouldn't perpetuate the fatphobia myths, but I could show her how harmful fatphobia can be. I told her about how people were killing themselves, getting divorced, giving up—all because of the pressures caused by fatphobia. I told her being fat wasn't a joke, but that didn't mean you couldn't approach it with a sense of humor. Now she was interested. I told her that only when you can laugh at the absurdity of fatphobia stereotypes can you put things into their proper perspective. I told her fat people must stop laughing at themselves and start laughing at the pettiness of other people.

I think this reporter went away with a better understanding of our problem, because the story I told in the interview was a positive one. By looking at a situation in a slightly different way I was able to change my thinking and, in turn, change the thinking of another person.

Photo courtesy of Lane Bryant.

Chapter 12

FATPHOBIA AWARENESS TRAINING:
Finally Something That Works

Carla begins **The Third Meeting** by handing out a quiz. Take it and see how much you know about fatphobia fact and fiction. Mark the statements you think are true.

1. Fat people are neurotic.
2. Having babies makes you fat.
3. Certain people are predisposed to obesity.
4. You usually gain weight if you stop smoking.
5. Certain traditionally sedentary jobs tend to make people fat.
6. Losing the first ten pounds is the easiest because it's mostly water weight.
7. You'll get sick if you don't eat enough of certain nutrients.

8. Food that tastes good is always fattening.

9. Certain combinations of food have special fat-burning properties.

10. The taste buds of fat people are more highly evolved.

11. Many fat people have sluggish metabolisms.

12. Fat people eat because they have empty lives.

Carla explained, "No matter what you answered, you are correct. There isn't enough evidence to prove or disprove any of these statements. Like all myths, there is a grain of truth hidden in the origin of each. It's up to us to find the small grain of truth hidden in these fatphobia myths so we can dispel them. According to the systems approach taught in many management science courses, a change in one part of a system causes the rest of the system to change. That's exactly what we want. When Carole Shaw, editor of **Big, Beautiful Woman** magazine, was asked what big women can do to feel better about themselves, she replied, "You've got to change yourself. You can't wait for the world to change. You've got to change it." In other words, if we change, the rest of the system has to change.

"We're talking about becoming better human resource managers. We all may have valuable resources going to waste. If we start using those resources instead of worrying about our body size, we could accomplish anything we put our minds to.

"It usually helps to write your thoughts down when you're working on attitude redirection. Even though it can be a nuisance, it really helps you see things more clearly. That's why we're going to use lesson plans for each meeting. Meetings without some structure are a waste of everyone's time. To avoid digressions, we'll use a six step system for problem-solving.

Step 1: Define your objective or problem.

Step 2: Do your research.

Step 3: Analyze your research.

Awareness Training

Step 4: Explore possible solutions and formulate a plan.

Step 5: Put your plan into action.

Step 6: Review your results.

"Apply these steps to a discussion of why diets don't work. When you join a FAT group like this, you expect to talk about behavior modification, exercise, nutrition, and diets. The average secretary probably knows more about nutrition and dieting than the average doctor. The reason our secretary knows so much about these subjects is because a large number of commercial interest have a big investment in her knowledge about these matters. Our loss is literally their gain. Take away the fancy packaging diets are wrapped in and you are left with a simple truth. If you want a smaller body, you have to eat less or exercise more. Diets exist because we've been brainwashed into thinking a smaller body is the answer to our problems.

"In a way, diets do work. If your only goal is to reduce your body size, diets restrict your calorie intake so that you eventually lose weight. As long as you consume fewer calories than you burn, you'll lose weight. Diets change your eating habits temporarily. They don't change your attitude, which is the basis for a permanent change.

"Diets fail because they don't take individual differences into consideration. Our eating habits and disorders are as unique as our fingerprints. Some people are meant to be bigger than other people. Being big isn't a crime. You don't have to be a glutton to be big. Heredity, environment, nutrition, and your health all contribute to your size. The main reason diets don't work is because we like to eat. In fact, eating should be a pleasurable activity. We need to stop punishing ourselves by setting ourselves up for failure.

"Diets can't help you stay thin forever. The more diets you've been on, the more you expect each one to fail. Instead of losing confidence in the dieting process, we lose confidence in ourselves. The more often we try to diet, the more feeble our willpower and endurance becomes. Nothing as uncomfortable and time-consuming as dieting can be a lasting cure for overeating. Any cure that leaves you obsessed with food intake and body size cannot be the answer.

"Diets restrict food intake. They don't deal with the origins of the problem. If overeating were simply a problem of taking in too many calories due to ignorance of nutrition, we would all be thin. Fat serves a function in our lives. It creates a cushion against life's blows. Fat helps protect us from life's disappointments. Fat is a scapegoat and an excuse for not succeeding. Eating gives us the strokes that no one else can or will give. Until we recognize fat serves all these purposes, we can't come to terms with our compulsive eating. Fat is just an adjective—we give it the power to limit our lives. When we take the power away from the fat, we can regain control of our eating and our lives.

"Doctors, friends, family, the scale, guilt, threats, and self-hatred are the jailers in our diet prisons. We restrict and repress until the temptation becomes so great we escape our diet prisons with a fullblown jailbreak binge. Every time we fall off the wagon, it's harder to climb back on. Each time we fail, we feel more guilty, more inadequate, more out of control. To make it worse, guilt prevents you from enjoying the food you eat on your binge.

Being thin often becomes a constant trade-off. The consequence can be the yo-yo syndrome. You try to maintain an unrealist level of thinness that sets you up for failure. Your weight goes up and down just like a yo yo. If you are dieting to be healthy, you should consider the fact that the yo yo syndrome has been found to be more dangerous to your health than staying at one weight, even if your weight is higher than what is considered to be socially acceptable.

"Diets don't stop compulsive eating, they encourage it. Diets make us powerless. They take away the ability to control our eating naturally. They make us stop trusting our judgment and the signals our body gives us. Compulsive eaters use food to solve non-food problems. That's why restricting your food intake won't stop your compulsive eating. That will

Awareness Training

only happen when you find other ways to deal with the stress that makes you rely on food in the first place.

"Dieting means abiding by rules and regulations that are constant reminders we can't be trusted. Being on a diet means you exist outside the mainstream of life. Dieting reinforces our compulsive behavior. It emphasizes fat and thin stereotypes. We can't isolate our eating habits and attitudes from the rest of our personality. Dieting doesn't help us get in touch with our attitudes about food, our eating habits, or our feelings about ourselves and others.

"We have to break our food addiction and learn to distinguish between real hunger and pseudo-hunger. Relaxation techniques, behavior modification, setting goals, heightened awareness, and learning to deal with our problems will help us overcome compulsive eating. Diets won't, because their magic is only temporary. Diets don't improve our lives, we do. Diets don't work because they put food at the center of your life." They are a temporary, artificial solution. Carla's lesson was followed by a spirited discussion.

> **Edna:** "Maybe I'd feel better at the end of the diet if I knew the weight would stay off. The statistics show 90 percent gain it back. It makes you wonder what your chances are of keeping it off. I have a fear of struggling for nothing, so why bother. They tell you that you'll have to diet for the rest of your life. The fat cells are there and will always be there. There's no way to get rid of them, so it's a losing battle."
>
> **Sue:** "The problem I have is that I'm at my goal, and now what? I couldn't wait till I got here; now I'm here and what's the big deal? Where is my sense of achievement? I think I'll gain five pounds and lose it again for something to do."
>
> **Jane:** "I gained twenty-five pounds and I went to the doctor for pills. I found that they didn't work anymore. They just aren't the answer, because you still don't learn to eat right."
>
> **Edna:** "Frustration, boredom, not losing weight, eating the same food every day, big event coming up—'that's what makes me

go off a diet. When you're faced with losing as much weight as I have to lose, it's like beginning a losing battle. You feel like it will take years. A pound a week doesn't do it. If I can't lose twenty-five pounds a month, I won't want to start. I could lose twenty-five pounds and no one would notice."

Kay: "Diets fail because of the person. It's hard when you're working. I have to go on business lunches, tours of homes, or open houses and resist all the goodies. You have to plan and prepare when you're on a diet and I just don't have time."

Jane: "When you're on a diet, you spend so much time and energy on the food, that that's all you think about. Then you go off of it, and it's harder to get back on. Why do things that taste good have so many calories? Why can't celery have 500 calories?"

Heather: "If I go on an immediate starvation diet, I may drop five, six, or seven pounds a week. But that's at 500 calories a day. I become miserable. I can't stay on that. I want to kill anybody in sight. That's no way to live. I want to be like everybody else. I want to be with everyone if they're stopping to eat."

Debbie: "I suffered, went through hell for a whole year, and I got the weight off. What do I do? Put it all back on. I just want to die. You get so disgusted with yourself, you want to jump off the Bay Bridge. All my life it's been up and down, up and down. Very depressing, especially when you go to buy clothes."

The Fourth Meeting

The members were now eager to share their weekly success stories. Since our group was down to ten members, we decided to close the membership for the remainder of the meetings. Tonight there was a special excitement in the room because we were ready to attack the most feared subject, compulsive eating.

Carla began the lesson by explaining that "compulsive eating results from using food to solve non-food problems. Eating becomes so symbolic that we seldom eat just because we're hungry. Food gets mixed up with other areas of our lives, and it becomes our enemy. We both fear it and love it.

Awareness Training

We talk about food as if it were a drug, a poison, or a magic potion, instead of fuel for our bodies and a pleasure for our souls.

"How do you know if you're a compulsive eater? Do you eat when you're not physically hungry or when you're full? Do you sneak food while you're trying to diet? Do you spend most of your day thinking about food? Do you feel like your eating and your life are out of control? Do you wake up feeling awful about what you ate the day before? Do you hate how you look? If your answers to most of these questions is yes, then you're a compulsive eater.

"Compulsive eaters make up excuses for eating. They think strangers really care about what they eat, and they live in constant fear someone will catch them eating. Eating becomes chaotic, uncontrolled, self-destructive and, most of all, frightening. To make matters worse, your body becomes fat which betrays your attempt to keep your compulsive eating a secret. You find yourself dieting overtime just to stay acceptably thin. To solve her problem, the compulsive eater must separate her concern about body size from her compulsive behavior. We've seen how body size prejudices can be changed. Compulsive eating is a complex disorder that may require professional attention.

"In order to overcome compulsive eating we must understand whether we subconsciously want to be fat, don't want to be thin, or are using eating to solve non-hunger problems. It is possible to want to be large. Some women feel it's a sign of nurturing or a form of protection. You may not want to be thin. After all dealing with sexual harassment can be bothersome. You may be eating because you're lonely or have other emotional reasons. Until you understand the origins of your eating behavior, you'll never be able to overcome compulsive eating.

"As a coping mechanism, compulsive eating is doomed to failure. It is a symptom, not a solution. If we know we eat in response to emotional disturbances and environmental signals, we at least have the beginnings of a solution. When we can't distinguish between physical hunger and emotional needs, we're in trouble. We must expose the underlying problems so they can be resolved. Knowing what the problem is can be a tremendous relief.

"Food is life-sustaining. It has special significance. Food represents customs and brings back memories. We cannot ignore something that invades every part of our culture. We have to make peace with our compulsive eating by relearning how to use natural body signals that tell us when and what to eat.

"Diets can become moral straitjackets. The dieting process can become our new obsession. The biggest reason we overeat is because we deny ourselves the foods we love. We eat through a filter of fear and guilt, never allowing ourselves to enjoy the experience. That's why we are never satisfied. We never find out what we really like to eat or where or with whom. Despite what the commercials say, eating is not a sin. If you want to overcome compulsive eating, you have to stop treating it that way. You have the right to enjoy your food. The solution to your compulsive eating problem lies in striking a balance between satisfying our physical and emotional needs."

The discussion of compulsive eating that Carla's lesson sparked went on late into the night. The comments made reveal that compulsive eating is often a matter of degree. Sometimes there is a fine line between compulsive eating and overeating.

> **Sandy:** "I don't think of myself as a compulsive eater. I don't eat when I get mad or unhappy or sad. But if you give me a bowl of popcorn, I'll finish it down to the last kernel. Is that compulsive?"
>
> **Heather:** "I'm a compulsive overeater. I have been since I was about twelve. When I was twelve and thirteen, I had money from my paper route and babysitting. I would buy junk with it. Food is very important to me. I was a tomboy, and my best friend was a boy who was two years younger and who could eat anything. He often chose carrots. His father worked for a bakery, and he could go to the back of the truck and get things anytime. He shared

freely, but I think I must have eaten most of them. But I don't remember the feeling of bingeing."

Kay: "I've had days where I could eat a whole loaf of bread—first with cheese, then peanut butter and jelly, then toasted with cinnamon."

Sue: "I've done that when going out to dinner. You eat the French bread, and then you're stuffed by the time dinner comes. I'll eat the whole thing, but then I'm in agony. I usually overeat only when I go out to dinner. I don't just sit around the house and eat. I don't hide cookies under the bed. I remember reading about this guy who kept cookies in the bathroom linen closet. I have't reached that point where I have to hide food and eat it somewhere else."

The Fifth Meeting

This marks our fifth week together. For the first time since we began, several members didn't want to share their success stories. Last week's discussion made a few people examine their lives more closely. Carla reminds us to call one another if we start feeling overwhelmed or alone. Carla is a good leader. This is her fifth FAT group, and she knows that now is the time for action. She doesn't want the group to dwell on negatives for too long, so this week's lesson is short. Most of the evening is devoted to games and tests that help us get control of our eating.

"Your body probably has more sense than you do. It tells you when it's being abused. It tells you when it needs something. We work very hard at trying to ignore those needs, especially when it comes to eating. Years of fatphobic thinking have made us distrust our bodies. We are so brainwashed, we don't know what normal means anymore.

"We're looking for our natural body weight, a level that's probably predetermined by our heredity. Our environment plays an important part in whether we'll reach that natural body weight. The only way to find this level is to listen to your hunger cues.

"Thin people who say they can eat anything and maintain their weight aren't lying. Once we develop a satisfying, stable, relaxed relationship with food, we will be able to say the same thing. Eating can be a sensuous experience, so why waste it on food you don't like? Don't worry, you won't become malnourished just because you allow yourself to eat the foods you like. In fact, you'll probably be improving your eating, because having the freedom to eat also means you have the freedom **not** to eat."

I'm not sure the exercises following the lesson proved anything scientific, but they were fun. For instance, I didn't realize different areas of the tongue were stimulated by different things: the front of the tongue is sensitive to sweet and cold; the rest of it is sensitive to sour, salty, and spicy.

EXERCISE 1. Are you an introvert or an extrovert? According to an experiment conducted at Cambridge University, if placing several drops of lemon juice on someone's tongue makes their mouth water a great deal, they are an extrovert. Is this true for you in your group?

EXERCISE 2. Focusing on Food. Arrange to bring a variety of foods to your meeting. Be sure to include foods that are salty, sweet, creamy, crunchy and, as many other textures and tastes as you can think of. Each person should sample each food. The group should be seated in a circle and facing outward. Close your eyes and slowly taste each food. Hold each sample in your mouth, feel it with your tongue, play with it. Don't be embarrassed. This is part of learning how you really feel about food. Think about this exercise when you next eat. Are you receiving full pleasure out of the food you eat?

I plan to repeat this exercise because it helped me get in touch with the foods I want but have been denying myself.

EXERCISE 3. I live in a supermarket. Visualize your house as a supermarket. What kinds of food would you stock on your shelves? Be honest. The list you compile will tell you what foods you really love.

These are some of the comments that resulted from this lesson. Each group member suggested one way to control compulsive eating.

Jane: "Stop dieting because diets don't work. Nothing awful will happen."

Sandy: "Give yourself permission to eat whenever you like, forever. Stop depriving yourself, because it just makes you want certain forbidden things more."

Barbara: "Learn to tell when you are physically hungry and when you are full."

Sue: "If you have a craving for a certain food, let yourself have it instead of denying yourself. Let yourself eat enough of the food to satisfy you so you won't want more later."

Debbie: "If you want to, allow yourself to eat unusual foods like breakfast at night."

Edna: "Taste each mouthful of food. Try to enjoy each flavor to its fullest. You'll eat less and enjoy it more."

Kay: "Stop during meals to see if you're full yet."

Heather: "Learn to leave food on your plate if you're full. Don't always try to clean your plate."

The Sixth Meeting

In the last few meetings, we seem to have broken some invisible barrier. The group has begun to share things freely. The success stories that begin each meeting are taking on new meaning. Instead of brief comments about what we didn't eat, members are beginning to explore their feelings about being fat.

It's so quiet, you can hear the ticking of the kitchen clock as Carla begins the lesson.

"A scale is like a slot machine. We keep putting time and money in, hoping for the numbers that will change our lives. Maybe it works for some people, but for most of us, it's never going to happen.

"I've finally found the perfect use for my scale—I use it for a plant stand. Expensive scales don't work any better than diets do in helping you lose weight. If you have to rely on a mechanical device to remind you that you're acceptable, you're totally out of touch with your body. Scales are external controls. We need to learn internal controls.

"Hunger isn't a punishment, it's a natural response to a legitimate need. You have to get back in touch with what real, physical hunger feels like. Hunger can trigger strong emotional responses. I become anxious when I'm hungry, some people get depressed. Learn to separate the emotion from the physical need. Let your body become your best friend. Take care of it, listen to it, and it will take care of you. It could take awhile to change compulsive eating patterns. It can be done. I've done it. I've met dozens of other women who have done it. With a little practice, you'll be able to recognize and satisfy true hunger. Now I can adjust my weight without using a scale. Whenever my eating habits get sloppy, I pay more careful attention to my hunger signals. Before I know it, I've dropped back into my normal weight range.

"To break your addiction to food, you have to relax. You have to become aware of what eating means to you. You have to learn to enjoy food in a normal, non-compulsive way. One way to become more aware of when and what you eat is to pay particular attention to your surroundings. Where and when is it most comfortable for you to eat? What eating situations make you uncomfortable? I found I don't like to eat at restaurants where you're seated with strangers. How about you?"

After the lesson, members of the group shared their experiences with food.

> **Barbara:** "I got really angry one day when my husband's partner was on the phone. I hung up on him, and I found myself wanting to eat something. that was my first time I realized I ate because of my emotions."
>
> **Debbie:** "Everything is centered around food, no matter what you do. Everywhere you go—movie, ballgame, or camping—there's food. You have people over and there are snacks. No matter what you do, it's associated with food. Name

one activity that is not in some way centered around food. Swimming? We usually have sandwiches or watermelon by the pool."

Edna: "I know my little tricks. I won't take one big plate of food, I'll take a small one and then keep going back for more. Or with cake, I'll start with little pieces. I know what I'm doing. I'm trying to act like I'm not eating two pieces of cake. I take ten cups of soup instead of one or two big bowls. The same with ice cream. So I see what I'm doing."

The Seventh Meeting

By the seventh week, we had the routine down pat. Now it was time to start acknowledging what motivates our behavior. We had to start questioning the information we were basing our attitudes and behavior on.

For this lesson, Carla read a list of facts and opinions she had collected in her research.

• Dr. Thaddeus Danowski, of the University of Pittsburgh, claims that when calorie intake is reduced to 500 calories less than the body needs to maintain its current weight, the body's thermostat is turned down and that lowers the basal metabolic rate. This mechanism is supposed to have helped us live longer when food was in short supply.

• Social psychologist Richard E. Nisbeth thinks that the body probably stores a predetermined amount of fat. The body automatically adjusts your food intake to maintain that set level. If this is true, the hypothalamus signal triggers your hunger signals in order to maintain the right level. Maybe that's why we get so ravenously hungry when we try to diet.

• Famous weight expert, Dr. Hilde Bruch, says if you get used to a weight and you seem to stay there naturally, that's probably the right weight for your body and lifestyle. What's important is not what you weigh, but whether you feel good and whether your body is in good working order.

• Some researchers contend fat people start out with normal metabolisms but their abnormal eating habits change their metabolic rate. Many experts don't believe low metabolism exists. Several studies have shown that fat people need fewer calories to maintain their weight.

• One doctor claims that fat people who reduce to "normal" size still need fewer calories than those who have never been fat.

• The American Medical Association says that only 5 percent of all cases of obesity are caused by metabolic disorders.

• Some scientists suggest a link between a high amount of endorphin, a morphine-like hormone produced by the body and fat in animals. Maybe we get a natural high from being fat.

• Dr. Mario De Luise, of Harvard University, discovered that some fat people have below-normal levels of an enzyme called sodium/potassium ATPase. ATPase helps burn off up to 40 percent of the calories not used in normal activities. If fat people have less ATPase, it might prove that some people do have slower metabolisms.

• One group of scientists suggest that a special kind of fat, called "brown fat," burns off calories more quickly than regular fat. People who are fat from birth are thought to have less brown fat.

• One popular theory has it that we can actually increase the number of fat cells we have by overeating during infancy and the preteen years.

• Barbara Reed, a probation officer, claims that too much sugar can make women lose their ability to reason, which can lead them to commit crimes they aren't even aware they're committing.

We then discussed how Carla's findings did or did not pertain to our lives.

Heather: "I really don't feel that what I eat justifies my weight. I don't use sugar. I drink Tab. I use so many substitutes. It's so frustrating, because I do cut out a lot of calories."

Sue: "I had a roommate, a little gal, whose bedtime snack was a bag of potato chips, French onion dip, and a quart of Pepsi.

This was her midnight snack, forget the two hamburgers, fries and a milkshake she put away at lunch. She always ate like that. My lunch would be one hamburger, fries, a Tab, maybe a couple of chips with the dip on them, and no Pepsi. I'd think, 'This isn't right, this isn't fair. I'm as active as she is.' That's probably my major gripe. How can someone sit around and eat more than I do and maintain a slender figure?"

Edna: "I had my daughter on a diet. I don't think she lost more than eight pounds in seven months. It was a struggle. There was nothing fattening in this house. My husband cooperated with me on that. I knew she couldn't blow it. If you're sticking to a diet and not having much success, doesn't that tell you something? Maybe you're just supposed to be that way?"

Jane: "How could my mother give birth to me and then give birth to them? Here they are: beautiful, thin babies. And I have to be fat all my life. I hated it. I hated every moment of it."

The Eighth Meeting

By the eighth meeting we were actually applauding each other's weekly accomplishments. Not the forced, phony applause you're obligated to give at certain diet groups, but an expression of genuine, enthusiastic appreciation. Most of us came to this meeting prepared to hear the typical song-and-dance about nutrition. Fortunately Carla had done her homework.

Her lesson was simple and our discussion was lively. At the end of the evening, she told us the only correct answer about what's good and bad for our bodies has to be based on our informed judgment. I think we'll all listen a little more carefully to the claims being made by so-called nutrition and diet experts. Maybe some of us will even take a nutrition class at the local junior college.

"I'm not against people making their bodies smaller. If being smaller will help you accomplish your goals, great. But if staying thin is a full-time job, maye it's time for you to question your occupation. If your self-esteem depends on a certain body size, what happens when it changes? Will your whole self-image fall apart?

"Every so often, I get the urge to indulge in a week of cottage cheese and carrot sticks. I understand how hard it is to give up dieting. If you must eat by a food plan, at least make it one that is good for you.

"You should be able to tell when you're gaining weight because your clothes will fit more snugly. Your body will feel heavier. It may be harder for you to move around. When you lose weight, your clothing gets looser. Your body feels lighter and it's easier to move around.

"At first, I was concerned that this kind of internal weight control wouldn't work. As I found better ways of dealing with my problems, I stopped using food to comfort myself. I began listening to my body signals carefully. I ate exactly what I wanted, and I ate until I felt full. My weight slowly dropped to 195 pounds, and I've stayed there for over two years. It's the first two years of my life when I haven't gained. Staying at the same weight is heaven. It's like being the perfect size 8 and being able to eat anything I want. Who cares if there's a one in front of that eight?

"I studied nutrition in college hoping to find the secret to permanent weight control. Instead of finding a cure, I found we don't really know much about nutrition. Sure we know more than we did even eighty years ago, but most research takes the form of experiments with animals. It's hard to tell exactly how the information gained from animal studies relates to human nutrition.

"The average American woman is becoming a pop nutrition expert, but she doesn't know the facts. We don't know and the experts don't know. Yet we try drastic cures, in the form of fad diets, without realizing what harm the diet could do to our bodies twenty years from now. Wild fluctuations in weight can be more dangerous to your health than maintaining a higher, but stable, weight. Malnourishment isn't good for your body, no matter how chic it makes you look. The U.S. Department of Agriculture's **Dietary Guidelines for Americans** advises:

1. Eat a variety of foods, including something from each of the four food groups.

2. Try to maintain an ideal weight.
3. Avoid eating an excess of fat, sugar, and salt.
4. Include natural bulk and fiber in your diet.
5. Drink in moderation, and don't smoke.

Unfortunately, the government isn't too sure what an ideal weight for everyone is so I'd amend that suggestion to read "Try to maintain your weight at one comfortable level."

The Last Meeting

Our final meeting. We each had mixed emotions. Some of us decided to continue in another of Carla's groups. Two of the members wanted to start their own groups. The rest will continue working on our own.

"Of all the topics that we discussed in our FAT group, the one that concerned people the most was whether being fat really is unhealthy. We hear a lot about how being overweight can shorten your lifespan or lead to all kinds of diseases and problems. Are these findings true?

"I'm not a doctor, so I really can't tell you whether fat is bad for you, but I don't think doctors can tell you either. New evidence indicates that all the fuss over fat may be greatly exaggerated. I always did think it was rather strange that adding lead weights to your belt when you run would make you stronger, carrying a few extra pounds of fat would make you sick.

"That's just the first of many contradictions you'll encounter when you research the medical issues. One doctor says the heart attack rate for fat people is down, another says it's up. You have to sort through this mass of information and make the decision for yourself.

"This is a sampling of the different medical facts and opinions I've uncovered:

- An underactive thyroid gland can cause a person to be sluggish and oversensitive to cold, have brittle nails, dry skin, thin hair.

It can also make them fat. Most of us don't have thyroid problems, though.

- When a woman's body fat level drops below 20 percent of her total weight, she may become amenorrheic (stop menstruating).

- People with Prader-Willi Syndrome can't stop eating. Only locked cupboards will stop the victims of this disease from eating everything in sight.

- The closest thing to hard evidence that links fat with health risk is hypertension has been correlated with being overweight. It has also been associated with heart disease.

- The National Center for Health Statistics claimed that 1,019 deaths in 1978 were directly attributable to obesity.

- If you have high blood pressure (hypertension), diabetes, or are planning to have surgery, you should lose weight if your doctor feels it's necessary.

- A preoccupation with weight and body size can cause anorexia nervosa, an eating disorder which can result in starvation; and bulimia, an eating disorder in which the victim alternately gorges and vomits. Fifteen to seventeen percent of anorexics will die.

- There is an 11 percent fatality rate for intestinal bypass surgery. Those who have bypass operations may also suffer liver and kidney damage, and cardiac arrest.

- In addition to causing some deaths, liquid protein diets can cause heart problems.

- According to Drs. Tepperman, Scepesi, each time your weight goes up, your blood cholesterol level rises.

- Overzealous dieting has been associated with high cholesterol levels, depression, gout, sleeplessness, malnutrition, anxiety, tension, heart disease, arthritis, kidney failure, gall bladder disorders, and death.

- The Third International Congress on Obesity held in Rome recently concluded there is no new solution for obesity. Instead of a cure for obesity, the conferees feel that working for remission, a period of time during which the symptoms of a condition are stabilized, is the best answer.

- Dr. Frank W. Barr's survey at Northwestern University showed people who are 25 to 35 percent overweight have the lowest mortality rate. Dr. Reubin Andres, a professor at Johns Hopkins University Medical School, says being moderately overweight is good for you. Dr. Ancel Keys says, "the issue of overweight has been vastly overblown." David Levitsky, a Cornell University nutritional scientist, thinks you can be 30 percent overweight and still be healthy.

- Dr. Andres found sixteen studies that indicate no relationship between overweight and an early death.

- Dr. Paul Scholten, a former president of the San Francisco Medical Society, said, "stop worrying about girth and focus on your worth."

- Famous heart transplant pioneer, Dr. Christiaan Barnard, thinks people should worry about the quality, as well as the quantity, of life. "If heavy people are made unhappy by strict diets, does the end result justify the misery?"

- Dr. Penny Wise Budoff has found overweight women have fewer problems with menopause.

Carla continued, "I can't tell you which of these statements is true. You'll have to research them and decide for yourself. I can tell you what I think of doctors and the way they treat fat people.

"I don't know how you feel about your doctor, but I'm tired of always being told that whatever is wrong with me is due to my weight. I resent having a doctor look down my throat and in my ears, only to tell me that losing fifty pounds is the cure for what ails me. Other women have had similar experiences.

"If, after extensive testing, a doctor told me that I'd developed a condition in which my weight was a factor, I'd reduce. I'm no dummy, I want to live. I'd want some pretty specific reasons for his advice. 'You'll feel better,' or

'It's better for you' won't do. I might even get a second opinion. Before I'd follow my doctor's advice, I'd consider whether I was really ready to get thin.

"Losing weight is relatively easy; keeping it off is the hard part. Even in a life-threatening situation, I'd want to work through the process as slowly as possible. Changing your body image is the prerequisite for permanent weight loss, and you can't change your body image overnight. It takes time to stop believing in the old fatphobia myths. But once you no longer believe them, no matter what size body you end up with, you'll have discovered a unique, happy person."

Carla's discussion of doctors and health elicited these responses from the group:

Edna: "Last year, when my daughter was fourteen, she had her appendix out. She was maybe ten pounds overweight. On her chart, the doctor wrote, 'very obese fourteen-year-old.' Who decides what's obese?"

Sandy: "A doctor told me, and she was a skinny little thing, that 'eating is strictly a social habit. When you go out to lunch with the girls, just have a cup of coffee—you'll lose weight'."

Kay: "I can remember going to see a doctor, a woman. I thought I would be more comfortable with a woman. The first thing she said when I walked in was 'Oh, my God, look at that fat. You're going to have to get rid of that. Look at all that blubber around your stomach.' "

Sue: "In the last year and a half, I've exercised much more. It's a total reversal of before. I'm still heavy, but it's your attitude that counts. Now I can walk a couple of miles."

Barbara: "The major reason why I lose weight, if I ever do, is because of my health. I'm only thirty-three, yet there are times when I feel sixty. I can't carry this weight much longer. And on top of that, I'm a smoker. I feel I'm endangering myself twice as much. I get very tired. Just sitting on the floor and getting up is a major ordeal. Walking up stairs. Even getting up off the couch. I think it really slows me down. I even went as far as checking out a bypass operation. I went for a test, talked to the psychiatrist, and even had the barium enema—the whole thing—as degrading as it was for me. The doctor gave me a list of six or seven people, and said before I went through with this I should talk to these people. Most of them were happy, but the ones who were unhappy were **really** unhappy. So I said to myself, 'Okay, you have got three choices: you can have it, you can jump off the Bay Bridge, or you can learn to accept yourself the way you are.' I've almost come to grips with the last choice, but I'm not sure I'll ever accept myself fully as I am. There's always that thing in the back of mind that someday, someday, I'll be thin. I realize that probably won't happen, but I won't give up. I'm still trying."

I'm sitting at my typewriter with chipped fingernail polish and limp hair, but I still feel beautiful. I've finally found the person I've always wanted to be. I have to admit that this person didn't come in a package the size I expected, but I've learned that size doesn't matter. I haven't stopped growing just because I feel good about myself. I look forward to the new challenges I've yet to face in the struggle to know myself better. I still have anxious days. I still overeat occasionally, but I'm totally aware of it when and why I do. I give myself permission to be human. I'm in control, but I'm not a tyrant. Be nice to yourself because you're your own best investment.

Don't let your bathroom scale become the judge of your self-worth. If you want to be healthy, that's great. If you tell me you have to be thin to be healthy, I disagree. Fat doesn't automatically mean you're not healthy any more than being thin automatically means you are.

If you say you want to be attractive, I'll applaud. Everyone should want to look and feel their best. If you tell me you have to be thin to be attractive, I'll disagree again. Fat and ugly aren't synonymous. I've known a lot of ugly people disguised in beautiful bodies. Give it a try. You, too, can become big and beautiful.

 FAT Groups are so new that we haven't had an opportunity to discover their full potential. I'm still collecting data on group experiences. If you'd like a reading list or if you would like to share techniques and experiences, please send a stamped, self-addressed envelope to me at Ruthanne Olds, Dept. 7,— Willowick Park Suite #180, 1170 Burnett Ave., #B, Concord, CA. 94520.

Photo courtesy of Lady Annabelle Lingerie, Inc.

Appendix A:
Exactly What A FAT Group Can Do For You

Exactly what can a FAT group do for you?

What are the goals a Fatphobia Awareness Training (FAT) group should strive for?

1. To use your intelligence rather than blindly following someone else's advice.

    A. To break a complicated subject down into manageable parts.

    B. To stimulate your thinking so you can come up with creative solutions to old problems.

2. To stop procrastinating and set aside a time to work on problems.

    A. To give you the company of those who share your pain, exhilaration, and indecision. To applaud the new opportunities that accompany your growth.

    B. To release the energy you usually invest in worrying about your weight for more productive uses.

3. To help you see that giving up fatphobia and compulsive eating is a gradual process involving your mental and physical selves.

    A. To help you get through the scary parts.

    B. To teach you alternative ways of coping with the problems that cause compulsive eating.

4. To stop letting your mind limit your potential.

   A. To encourage you to question everything you've ever heard or read about fat.

   B. To allow you to look at the world in new ways.

   C. To give you the courage to try new ways of doing things.

   D. To uncover your hidden strengths.

   E. To increase your self-esteem by increasing your ability to experience satisfaction.

5. To help you inventory your life so you can feel more comfortable with your choice.

   A. To feel better about your physical self.

   B. To feel better about your relationships.

   C. To feel better about your career.

   D. To feel better about your communication skills.

   E. To feel better about your place in the world.

   F. To feel better about your ability to enjoy the here and now.

6. To overcome compulsive eating by self-acceptance and non-dieting.

   A. To learn why your past efforts have failed.

   B. To explore conflicts related to eating and weight.

   C. To learn techniques for losing weight permanently, if that's what you **want**, without diets or scales, while eating your favorite foods.

   D. To help you get back in touch with your body, so you can respond to its signals.

   E. To uncover and demystify the various symbolic meanings of fat and thin.

F. To learn new ways to deal with food and hunger by overcoming years of conditioning to certain foods as negative and others as positive.

7. To make you active in the fight against fatphobia.

   A. To increase your awareness of how fatphobia affects your life.

   B. To teach you how to break through the years of training that limits your potential.

   C. To help you see that fatphobia is a universal problem.

   D. To improve the world by improving our lives.

Group leaders should make copies of this list and send it to prospective members before the first meeting.

The First Meeting

At your first FAT group meeting, you should determine the group's structure and function. Without these two essentials, the group cannot achieve its goal. A lack of direction encourages friction, boredom, and disappointment. During the first meeting, you should also decide on:

Number of Members. It's best to specify a limit. The ideal group has between five and ten members, but you may want to start with more, since some people will drop out. A small group permits intimacy and variety. New members should not be accepted after the third meeting. The member of a group cannot learn to trust each other if there are different members present each week.

Each member must make a commitment to attend every meeting. Only one excused absence should be allowed. Any member who misses a second meeting should be dropped. This may sound strict, but if you're serious about working on a problem, you have to be serious about attending the meetings. If a member has to be dropped he or she should be encouraged to join another group when they can commit an uninterrupted block of time.

The question of whether men or good friends of other members should be allowed to join your group must also be addressed.

Confrontation Members should strive to be non-judgmental in response to other members' experiences. Confrontation should only be allowed in the confines of an exercise. It's up to each member to confront him or herself on the issues. Other members can't guess the real meaning of someone's statement. Members should avoid arguing, justifying, explaining, challenging, prodding, or putting others down. Instead, everyone should learn the art of active listening.

Meeting Time. Decide on a specific number of meetings, eight to ten is about average for a group of this kind. If you want to continue after you've finished the agreed on eight or ten meetings, you can either plan another series of meetings or form other groups. If everyone in your group wants to continue, then, by all means, do so.

Decide on beginning and ending times and stick to them. Two-hour sessions give the members enough time to share but not enough time to get bored. The number of meetings per week will be determined by the availability of group members. Most groups find that meeting once or twice a week works best. Some groups may want to plan a weekend at a resort.

Select one home or location for your meetings. Changing the meeting place gives the group a feeling of having no home.

Confidentiality. It's hard to establish an open environment if people feel what they say will become public knowledge. Don't take issue of confidentiality lightly. Even if you disguise names and identities, the word has a way of getting around. Taking notes and making recordings, visitors, and guests shouldn't be allowed for the same reasons. Interested outsiders should be directed to another group. No observers should be allowed to sit in on a group in progress.

Dues. FAT Groups should be free unless the teacher has special experience and expertise. Money can be collected to cover such expenses as child care, refreshments, field trips, and special programs. These optional expenses should be negotiated as the group sees fit. FAT groups are not intended to be a profit-making business for the leaders. The selling of products and services at meetings should be strictly forbidden.

Officers. Every group has a leader, whether they're elected or not. All FAT groups should elect a leader at the first meeting. The person who organizes the first meeting usually plans to act as the leader. Leading a FAT group requires certain talents and carries certain responsibilities. (See the section on becoming a leader). Leading a group can be a rewarding experience, but it requires a commitment of time and energy. The success of a group often depends on the abilities of its leader, so choose carefully. Remember that the leader is not a hostess.

You may also want to elect meeting coordinators. If you decide to collect funds for various activities, you may need a treasurer. If you want to have special programs, you may need an events coordinator. These offices are optional offices that will be agreed upon by your group. Officers can be elected or simply volunteer, whichever works best for your group.

Program for the First Meeting. After you've decided on a structure for the group, you should discuss the group's goals. Refer to the list at the beginning of this appendix for help. Discuss the areas that seem most important to your group. The group doesn't have to adhere to these goals rigidly, but the list gives the group a starting point.

The remainder of the first meeting should be devoted to hearing everyone's fat story. The leader should review my fat story and prepare their fat story as an example for the rest of the group to follow. Sharing your fat story will help others understand what brought you to the group. When you discover how much you all have in common, everyone will start to relax.

The group is encouraged to share food at the end of each meeting. This will help everyone learn to use food in a normal way. Refreshment duties can be rotated or shared; they can be potluck or purchased with dues money.

A Typical Meeting

A typical FAT group would include the following:

- Introduction of meeting topic by leader.
- Review of ground rules, if necessary.
- Sharing of positive experiences. No member is required to participate (we all have bad weeks).
- A lesson read by the leader or played on a tape recorder.
- Responses to the opening question given by each member. Every member has the right to pass. Going around the circle gives each person time to talk and listen without feeling rushed or pressured.
- Open discussion on the leader's list of questions. The leader should keep the discussion moving in the right direction.
- Discussion moves from the personal level to a discussion of how the problem under consideration relates to the world.
- Exercises, if any.
- Summary of points covered and explanation of assignments for the next topic.

Becoming a Leader

A FAT group leader is not a dictator or a substitute-mother. She shouldn't be on an ego trip. She's a facilitator—a catalyst for the group's growth. Leaders are made, not born, so a leader must be willing to prepare for her role. A leader's first job is to organize her group. You have to be sure everyone understands the group's structure and function, but you're not responsible for knowing all the answers. You'll be growing along with the group. If you don't know something, admit it.

A leader should possess the following qualities:

- Warmth, openness, the ability to care

- Assertiveness and ability to guide conversation when it gets bogged down
- Commitment to reading, study, and researching
- Enthusiasm
- Ability to become part of the group
- Capacity for leadership
- Self-confidence and positive attitude
- Fairness
- Foresight—willing to prepare and plan for groups

The leader's job includes:

- Encouraging the full participation of all members without playing favorites, while respecting every member's right to pass.
- Controlling the environment so it's comfortable for everyone in the group.
- Guiding the discussion so people don't get hung-up on unimportant details. Reminding people that everyone has the right to talk. (Be on guard against people who try to take over the group.)
- Screening members to weed out those with potentially serious problems. (You may have to ask certain people to leave the group. Some people are just argumentative; others like to intimidate people to compensate for their inadequacies. These kinds of people will impede the progress of the other members.)
- Giving advice and solving problem. These are two different things. If a member asks for help in solving a problem, encourage the other members to relate any personal experiences that may be of use. Show a person their options, don't give them advice.
- Enforce all the rules. Groups that don't follow their rules usually don't succeed.

- Stick with it. Groups have moods just like the people. Don't take it personally if a group or meeting doesn't work out. You're all learning, and that's what really matters.

- Develop your own image. You'll be a role model for the other group members.

- Have enough lesson plans to last the entire eight-or ten-week session before you hold the first meeting. (See the section on lesson plans). Introduce your ideas for the group's approval. If the group wants to work on an area you haven't prepared, you should be willing to comply with their wishes.

- Keep up with any paperwork. If you have a large number of people wanting to be part of the group, you may have to devise an application form. You may have to handle the money for food, if your group doesn't have a treasurer. You may have to put an ad in the newspaper. After the first meeting, you should provide each member with a list of all the names and phone numbers. You'll need to distribute copies of the goals, sample first meeting, sample agenda, and your agenda for the first meeting before the group meets.

If fatphobia tends to isolate us, how will we find other people who want to participate in a FAT group? You can post notices on community bulletin boards, or you can advertise in the paper. A friend of mine ran this ad to start her group:

> HELP! PLEASE help me help myself. Free support group forming to understand my weight problem. No diets. No gimmicks. No cost. Just moral support and friendship. Sandi. (Her phone number.)

I started my groups by asking friends to invite one or two of their friends who might be interested. As the idea catches on, it will be easier to find interested people. Sandi had the devil of a time convincing people she wasn't trying to sell them some crazy diet or vitamins.

I know the thought of gathering people together to talk about our most secret problems may be a little frightening. I was afraid the first few times I entered a group of strangers. After we all shared our fat stories we laughed, cried, learned, and shared. When I stopped letting fatphobia get in my way, it was easy to form a group.

One time I attended two FAT Groups in one day. I was so full of energy, I wrote until 3 a.m. It was wonderful to be able to talk about things that have been hidden for too many years. It was nice to share the joy and the pain while we learned from each other. Lets learn how to use the FAT groups to help achieve a balance in our lives.

Developing a topic

I. Selecting a Topic

Define your objective or problem specifically. Condense the topic into a single statement or question. Start with a general idea. This helps focus the direction of the discussion. This helps focus the direction of the discussion.

You might start with a question like, "Why do I eat compulsively?" Think about all the aspects of the question. Is it too broad or too narrow for one discussion period? Our question about compulsive eating may be too broad, because we each eat for a variety of reasons. Narrow the question down, make it more specific, more focused. Ask why unfamiliar situations triggers compulsive eating? To be even more specific, ask why does meeting strangers make some people want to eat compulsive?

II. Research

Our research should uncover thought-provoking material and survey all available information. I like this part the best. Read, collect information, take classes, attend lectures, talk to people, and, when you can, interview the experts.

Let's return to narrowed-down version of our compulsive eating question. You might read articles and books on how to overcome the fear of the unknown. You might take a class designed to improve your communications skills and report the results to your group. You could talk to other people and find out how they overcame similar problems. Last but not least, you should review your past experiences and observe your current behavior as grist for the FAT group mill.

Don't forget to jot your findings down so you can share them with the group. It doesn't have to be formal, as long as you can organize your thinking, you'll be prepared for the meeting. Look always for the political, moral, logical, and emotional implications of your topics.

The way you present your research is a matter of personal style. You may want to present it as a short report. You may want several members to give shorter reports. You might even list a series of thought-provoking statistics and have the group try to relate them to personal experiences. Use your imagination to make your research come alive. People learn better when they are having fun.

III. Analysis

To get your group talking and thinking, prepare a list of questions before each meeting. For practice, add to the list of questions included in the sample topics. The more questions you have to draw from, the more confident you'll feel. Try to organize your questions logically, so you end by exploring how the topic relates to the world.

Questions you might include on your list are:

- Do you see a pattern of behavior?
- Where did the idea or attitude originate?
- How can we change it?
- What kind of a role does it assign us to?
- How does it affect our jobs, our lives, our relationships?
- Why is this happening?
- Who is in charge in this situation?
- How do the people in power use it to affect our lives?
- What would happen if things were suddenly different?
- Is the problem caused by an attitude that can be changed?

You may also want to develop exercises, games, and techniques, such as role playing, to help you analyze each topic. The more all your senses are involved in the learning process, the more meaningful the learning experience becomes.

IV. Exploring the Options

Examine alternatives, don't give advice. Your job is to encourage everyone in the group to see that they do have choices. They don't have to blindly accept the roles assigned to them because of fatphobia sterotypes. Stress that there are no right answers. Each person has to find out what will work for them.

If this part of the meeting bogs down, introduce the concept of time management. According to the theory of time management, you have three basic courses of action when faced with a task or problem: you can do the work yourself; pay someone else to do the work; or decide the task or problem isn't important and ignore it. Ask the group for suggestions on how they can solve the problem themselves, who they would pay to solve it, or how they can redirect their attitudes so the problem solves itself.

V. Putting Your Plan Into Action

I haven't included this step in my sample topics because each individual member has to devise her own plan of action. Members must help to solve their problems if they are to overcome compulsive eating and fatphobia. Once someone has a plan, they can call on other members for support and assistance in carrying it out. Encourage group interaction outside of the meetings. It can be a lonely world out there, especially when you are learning to cope in new ways.

VI. Evaluation and Feedback

Take ten or fifteen minutes of each meeting to review each member's progress in implementing their plan. It is important to recognize their accomplishments. We often expect so much of ourselves, we don't take the time to acknowledge what we have done. Encourage the group to applaud and cheer when a member reports a goal realized or a problem solved. We need all the support we can get.

First Meeting

Discussion Questions and Exercises

1. What kinds of self-motivation and self-improvement techniques have the group members tried?

2. Could any of the techniques discussed be used to overcome fatphobia? If so, how?

3. Do you think it's possible to change the system by changing yourself?

4. If you don't feel it's possible, how do customs and attitudes change?

5. If you do believe attitudes can be changed, what are some of the ways we can change people's ideas about us?

(The group leader or group members should feel free to add to this list of questions.)

EXERCISE 1: Affirmations

Affirmations are positive statements used in several self-help techniques that help redirect your attitudes. Take one affirmation from the following list and repeat it to yourself several times each day. Select a different one each day for the next week. At the next meeting, talk about whether these affirmations helped you change any attitudes. Did they change your behavior?

1. I have the right to be happy.

2. I have the ability to reach the goals I've set for myself.

3. I will stop blaming outside forces for my failures. I am responsible for my actions, good or bad.

4. I will find the lesson to be learned in each mistake I make.

5. I will not be afraid of the risk involved in reaching my goal.

6. I have the power to change fatphobia.

7. I deserve respect, so I will respect myself.

Appendix A

EXERCISE 2: Refrigerator Door Art

Sometimes I need to put my thinking into a two-dimensional form, particularly when it comes to sorting out my feelings about a complex subject like fatphobia. I'm not an artist—my drawing abilities are limited. So I use art and pictures from newspapers and magazines to create collages that express my feelings about a subject.

I started with a large sheet of posterboard and a picture of a jail cell. As I saw images I liked, I cut them out and added them to the collage. Sometimes I'd save several images before I'd go to work. Everytime I added an image that represented a part of my conflicting emotions, I'd concentrate on the feeling it evoked. Refrigerator door collages are one way of focusing your attention on the problems you'll encounter in your FAT group meetings. When I'm satisfied that a collage is done, I store it in my closet and start a new one. You can see from each collage how you've grown.

EXERCISE 3: I Am What I Am

This is a fun exercise that can be finished in your meeting. Copy the following on a large sheet of paper:

> If you feel _____
> You will look and act _____
> If you look _____
> You will feel and act _____
> If you act _____
> You will look and feel _____

Each member takes a turn filling in the blanks with an attitude she would like to develop. Read the statement first and then try to project the kind of image that would express the attitude. This can get outrageously funny, but no one said growing was always painful. It makes you think about how to connect your attitudes and your actions.

Putting Your Plan Into Action

You shouldn't expect the group to chart a course of action for you. This is where you have to take charge of your education. Your problems are unique, so your plan will be unique. Think about the options discussed in your group. Use them, change them, modify them—whatever works for you is the right answer.

Evaluation And Feedback

This step should be covered in the meeting following the discussion of the topic. Time is allowed in the sample agenda for members to share experiences relating to the previous week's work. This gives each member a chance to share their successes and failures. Due to time limitations, keep this part of the meeting short. You may be tempted to spend an entire meeting discussing the results of last week's work. Resist. Move on to another topic. If, at the end of your eight-to ten-week schedule, you wish to continue discussing with certain topics, schedule another series of meetings. Learning is a never ending process, so don't expect eight to ten meetings to solve all your fatphobia problems.

Second Meeting

Discussion Questions and Exercises

1. What is the relationship between dieting and bingeing in your life?

2. Why do you eat when you're not really hungry?

3. What kinds of situations make you overeat?

4. Why don't diets work for you?

5. Who benefits from our constant mania for thinness?

EXERCISE 1: How Much to Invest?

Dieting fuels a $10 billion-a-year industry. On a large sheet of paper, list the diet methods the group has tried in the last five years. List the total number of times each member has tried each plan and how much it cost them. Stop after you've listed a dozen or so, otherwise you might be there all day. Now total the costs, but be sure you're sitting down first. Some groups may find they could have bought a Mercedes with the money they've spent on diets.

EXERCISE 2: What Can I Do Besides Diet?
List the areas and the ways in which you could develop yourself without dieting. If you're shy, for example, then read a book on overcoming shyness or take a class on how to meet people. You could even take up a hobby that involves meeting people.

Putting Your Plan Into Action
Select one area in your life that needs improvement and where dieting won't help. Make plans to improve this area over the course of the next eight or ten weeks. Plan to tell the group about your project at the next meeting.

Evaluation and Feedback
Review each member's project plans.

Third Meeting

Discussion Questions
1. Why do you associate certain foods with certain events?
2. What would it be like to celebrate these events without the special kind of food? Is it wrong to place this kind of emphasis on food?
3. What does bingeing mean to you?
4. What makes you binge?
5. Can you tell the difference between physical and emotional hunger?
6. Why don't diets stop compulsive eating?

Exploring Options

Here are some possible ways to overcome compulsive eating:

1. Stop cold turkey.

2. Gradually stop by keeping busy with other things.

3. Find why we have the problem and then stop it.

4. Find better ways to deal with what causes compulsive eating and then stop it slowly.

5. Continue to eat compulsively and stop worrying about it. Enjoy the food, stop feeling guilty, and get on with the business of living.

Evaluation and Feedback

Each member should attempt to identify what triggered her last compulsive eating binge. She should be prepared to share how she felt when she realized the cause of her bingeing.

Fourth Meeting Exercises

EXERCISE 1. The One-Week Food Journal

Keep a food journal for one week to observe, not judge, your actions. Keep track of when and why, the what is your business. You're looking for patterns of behavior.

- Do you tend to eat alone or with other people? How do you feel about this? Would you like to change?

- Can you pinpoint the origin of your hunger? Does it feel like it comes from your stomach, mouth, throat?

- Do you watch TV, read, or talk while you are eating? Does this make the experience better or just less noticeable? Do you tend to focus on the food or the activity?

- Do you often eat things because of the time of day or the custom?

Appendix A

EXERCISE 2: You Deserve A Treat Today
Next time you reach for a snack, ask yourself,
"Would I rather have a(n) _____?
(Fill in the blank)

- Chat with a friend
- Nice fragrant bath
- Hour with a good book or magazine
- Window shopping trip with a friend
- Quiet time for myself
- Bite to eat—I'm really hungry.

EXERCISE 3: The Best Meal of My Life
Visualize the best meal of your life. Who would be invited? What would you serve? Where would you have it? Would it be possible? By sorting out the other needs you're mistaking for hunger, you'll be able to recognize real hunger when it strikes you.

Fifth Meeting

Discussion Questions and Exercises
1. Have you found you tend to return to the same weight when you relax and eat normally?
2. When did you first become fat?
3. Do you think consuming large amounts of sugar affects our behavior?
4. Which of these theories makes the most sense to you?

EXERCISE 1: Finding Your Calorie Requirement
Your BMR, or Basal metabolic rate, is the number of calories your body requires to perform basic life functions. Your body needs these calories even if you don't get out of bed all day.

To find your BMR, multiple your current weight by ten if you are moderately active, by twelve if you're very active. I weigh 195 pounds. If I multiply by ten its 1950 calories. That means it takes approximately 1950 calories a day to maintain my present body weight.

Sixth Meeting

Discussion Questions and Exercises

1. Is it possible to eat the foods you like and still be healthy
2. Do you think you can control your weight without a scale?
3. How can you be sure you aren't teaching your children to ignore the message their bodies give them?

EXERCISE 3: Rating the Diets

Make a chart comparing the nutritional value of several popular diets. Compare them to the suggested servings from each of the four food groups, or break them down further into individual nutritional elements. Several publications have done this kind of study. Look them up at the library. Consumer Guide's **Rating the Diets** is a good place to start.

Seventh Meeting

Discussion Questions

1. Why do the people who need to diet the least seem to be the most concerned about it?
2. Do you diet to be fashionable or healthy?
3. If obesity is a disease, why isn't it covered by most health insurance plans?

Exploring Options

- If you want to be healthy, try developing better habits. You don't need to change your body size to be healthy. Instead, stop

Appendix A

smoking, start exercising, get plenty of rest, and drink more water.

- Find a weight you can live with and stay there.

- If you don't have serious medical problems, don't create them by worrying too much about being overweight.

Photo courtesy of YOUNG STUFF a division of Stout Sportswear Group.

Appendix B: Other Topics

FATPHOBIA AND OUR THINKING.

- Why do I always feel so guilty about _____?
  (Fill in the blank)

- When will I stop apologizing for being big?

- How do I overcome the isolation caused by fatphobia?

- How do I motivate myself after so many failures?

- Who will take care of me while I'm taking care of my home, my family, and my husband?

- Would I still feel_____
  (depressed, lonely, angry) if I got thinner?   (Fill in the blank)

- Which comes first, self-hatred or rejection by others?

- What kind of emotional experiences contribute to my compulsive eating?

- Can charisma be learned?

- How do I build my self-confidence without becoming a snob?

- If I don't respect myself, who will?

- How do I survive my life crises without resorting to compulsive eating?

- How much does the labeling process contribute to fatphobia?

- Does being fat really make me different?

- How important is developing my body image in overcoming fatphobia?

FATPHOBIA AND OUR BODIES

- Are compulsive eaters neurotic?
- Have I lost touch with my body?
- Are there physical reasons for my depression?
- How nutritional are diets?
- Why do I substitute diet foods for real foods?
- If doctors, scientists, and researchers don't know much about metabolism, how much do they know about the connection between herdity and body size?
- Will exercise help me lose weight? What kind of exercise should fat people do?
- How do you cure anorexia nervosa and bulimia?
- Can I change my eating habits permanently?
- Is being thin worth the time, energy, and hassle?
- How do I handle people who won't accept my new eating habits.
- How can I encourage my children to heed their natural hunger signals?
- How do I deal with the problems that can arise when everyone in the house but me is eating naturally?

FATPHOBIA AND THE WORLD

- How much does the media affect my thinking about body size?
- What do I do if I think I'm being discriminated against because of my weight? Are fat people protected from discrimination as other minority groups are?
- Why does society romanticize certain destructive behavior patterns (e.g., workaholics and playboys), while it abhors fatness?

- Does being fat affect my relationships with friends, children, parents, spouse?
- Is fat a feminist issue?
- Fat power—how to get it, how to use it?
- Who makes us victims?
- Why does worrying about fat seem like a woman's problem, even though there are as many fat men as there are fat women?

Appendix C

*Directory of Stores
Where You Can Buy
Big, Beautiful Clothes*

This directory contains the names of stores throughout the United States that carry clothes in sizes 20 and above. Most major department stores and specialty shops carry up to size 20 or 24½ and half sizes now. Inclusion in this directory does not imply endorsement by either the author or the publisher.

ALABAMA
Birmingham
New Ideal
Parisian, Inc.
Pizitz

Dothan
Janice Williamson

Mobile
C.J. Gayfer

Montgomery
Gayfer's

ALASKA
Anchorage
The Sunflower Shoppe

Fairbanks
Queen Bee

ARIZONA
Maricopa
The Broadway Southwest

Phoenix
Big & Beautiful Shop
Diamond's
Lynn's Ladies Apparel

Tucson
May's
Whipple's

ARKANSAS
Little Rock
Gold's House of Fashion
Smart Size

Texarkana
Rayes

CALIFORNIA
Ella Nor's
Liberty House

Anaheim
Pant-Pouri

Aptos
Plum Pretty

Arcadia
Hinshaw's

Atascadero
Town & Country Fashions

Bakersfield
Malcolm Brock Co.

Bell
Modern Woman Stores

Bellflower
Miriam's

Beverly Hills
Camp Beverly Hills
The Forgotten Woman
Lane Bryant

Brawley
Country Casuals

Burbank
Mode O'Day Co.

Calexico
Garlan's

Costa Mesa
House of Terry
Nordstrom's

Culver City
Quist's II

Del Amo
Lane Bryant

El Cajon
Pretty & Plump

El Cerrito
Jerri B.

Escondido
Mercantile

Fresno
House of Large Sizes
Village East

Fullerton
Eleanor's Half Size

Hayward
Bert's
Mervyn's

Lakewood
Passy's

La Mesa
Woman's World

Los Angeles
Atlas West
Broadway
Bullock's
Clothes for Eve
Designers at Large
Frederick Atkins
Kline-Kinsler
Lane Bryant
The May Co.
J.C. Penney
Shelly's Tall Girl

Oakland
Emporium Capwell
Liberty House
Strom's

Palm Beach
Lane Bryant

Palo Alto
Bullock's

Placerville
Cash Mercantile

Redondo Beach
The Woman's Room

Redwood City
House of Large Sizes

Reseda
Millman's

Sacramento
California Apparel
Elegant Lady

San Bernardino
Lady Markells

San Diego
Walker Scott Co.

San Francisco
Bullock's
Emporium Capwell
Golden Gate
Lane Bryant
Liberty House
Macy's
Zoftig

Walnut Creek
Added Dimensions
Milady

Whittier
Hinshaw's

COLORADO
Denver
Joslin's

Pueblo
Vic Bains

CONNECTICUT
Hartford
Sage-Allen & Co.

New Haven
Exclusive Dress Shop

Norwich
Feister & Raucher

Orange
La Grande Boutique

DELAWARE
Wilmington
Braunstein's
Lovely Lady

DISTRICT OF COLUMBIA
Dana Robins
Full & Fancy (c/o Klein's)
The Hecht Co.
Pat Arnold's Talls
Sixteen Plus
Stylish Stout Sop
Woodward & Lothrop's

FLORIDA
Added Dimensions

Boca Raton
The Forgotten Woman
Truly You

Clearwater
Today's Woman

Ft. Lauderdale
The Forgotten Woman
Kern's
The Tram Shop
Wendy's Place

Miami
Burdines
Jordan Marsh
Lots to Love

Panama City
Leon's

Tampa
Maas Bros.

West Palm Beach
Truly You

Winter Haven
Erich's Inc.

GEORGIA
Added Dimensions

Atlanta
Davison's
Francesca
Lane Bryant
Lots to Love
Rich's

Augusta
Crosby's

Big &
Beautiful

Columbus
Kirven

La Grange
Solomon's

Marietta
Big Girl Fashions

Milledgeville
Goldstein's

HAWAII
Honolulu
Skirts 'n Blouses
The Trunk

Waipahu
Arakawas

ILLINOIS
Alton
Lee Anne

Belleville
Smith's Ready-to-Wear

Centralia
Foxy Lady

Chicago
Anne Brooks
Lane Bryant
Madigan's
Marshall Field
Pennington's
Sears Roebuck & Co.
Smart Size
Theresa's
Wieboldts

Chicago Heights
Hayman-Hawkins

East St. Louis
La Belle Shop

Evanston
Aparacor

Geneseo
Leading Lady

Gibson City
Rose Shoppe

Jerseyville
Bertman's

La Grange
Charles A. Stevens

Niles
Ann Brooks
Large World

River Forest
Madigan's

River Oaks
Lane Bryant

Rock Falls
Sowles

Rockford
Bergner/Weise

Skokie
Added Dimensions
Ladies at Large
Tall Styles

Springfield
Roland's

INDIANA
Indianapolis
L.S. Ayres
William H. Block Co.
B.J. Stout World
Smart Size

Muncie
Smart Size

Kokomo
J.J.'s Fashions

La Porte
Levine's

South Bend
Milady

Terre Haute
Root Dry Goods

Valparaiso
J. Lowenstine & Sons

Winamac
Miller's

IOWA
Burlington
J.S. Schramm

Cedar Rapids
Killian's

Cherokee
Hawley Allison Co.

Davenport
Petersen-Harned-Von Maur

Des Moines
Betty J's
Plus Shops

Oskaloosa
Sunflower

Ottumwa
Brody's

Shenandoah
Mae Farmer Fashion

Sioux City
Fantle's
Kalin's Coat & Furs

KENTUCKY
Paducah
Gwen's Stout Shop

LOUISIANA
Baton Rouge
Goudchaux's

New Orleans
D.H. Holmes
House of Broel
Krauss Co.
Lord's
Maison Blanche
Gus Mayer
The Vogue

MAINE
Williamsport
Dora Dale

MARYLAND
Baltimore
Herman Inc.
Hochschild Kohn
Hutzler's
Lane Bryant
Massey's
N. Schlossberg & Son

Langley Park
Ruth Rider

Pikesville
Pauline Moses (Plus)

Ridgely
Sachs & Co.

Rockville
Plus Sizes
Queen Size World

Salisbury
Bergers

MASSACHUSETTS
Athol
Muskovitz

Boston
Filene's
Jordan Marsh
Lane Bryant

Braintree
Lane Bryant

Great Barrington
The Chifforobe

MICHIGAN
Detroit
J.L. Hudson Co.
Smart Size

East Detroit
Kitty Kelly Shops, Inc.

Grand Rapids
Days Fashions, Inc.

Hamtramek
Lady Gentry

Jackson
Jacobsen's
Lane Bryant
Northland
Ruby's Inc.

Marine City
Priehs Dept. Store

Port Huron
Martha C.

Southfield
The Special Lady

Tecumseh
J.W. Milliken, Inc.

West Bloomfield
Willow Tree
Rogers Dept. Store, Inc.

Village
Sy's Unlimited

MINNESOTA
Albert Lea
The Picadilly Boutique

Austin
Queen Fasions

Edina
Home of Large Sizes

Fridley
House of Large Sizes

Minneapolis
Dayton's
House of Large Sizes Inc.
Sample Mart/Special Size Shop

Big & Beautiful

227

St. Cloud
Herberger's

Waconia
Van Arsdell's, Inc.

MISSISSIPPI
Anderson
Rust & Martin, Inc.

Clayton
Roth's

Florissant
Blattner's

Jackson
The Parisian

Woodville
Treppendahl Dry Goods, Inc.

MISSOURI
Columbia
Lorna's

Grandview
House of Large Sizes

St. Joseph
Paris Plus

St. Louis
Famous Barr
Lane Bryant
The Specialty Shops, Inc.

MONTANA
Billings
Dahl's

Helena
Kitzenberg Style Shop

Big &
Beautiful

228

NEBRASKA
Kearney
Hellman's Ready to Wear

Lincoln
Lots to Love

McCook
Lots to Love

Omaha
J.L. Brandeis & Sons, Inc.
Fashion at Large

NEVADA
Las Vegas
Lane Bryant

Reno
Pam's

NEW JERSEY
Bambergers

Bayonne
Paradise Shop

Elizabeth
The Special Woman

Englewood
Elaine Ames
Manhassat
Lane Bryant

Flemington
Added Dimensions

Fort Lee
The Forgotten Woman

Milburn
Jalm Boutique

Moonadie
Pennington's

Nutley
J.N.C.

Paramus
Corset Bar

NEW YORK
Astoria
Smart Size

Bayside
En Roto Boutique

Bronx
Schloss II
Smart Size

Brooklyn
Charisma
Smart Size

Buffalo
Adam, Meldrum & Anderson

Cedarhurst
Just Right

Great Neck
Daisy's Corner

Hudson Falls
J.W. Rhodes

Jamestown
Bigelow's Dept. Store

Latham
Interstate Dept. Stores

Liverpool
Stylish Woman Ltd.

Mamaronack
Beauti-Full Size

Manhasset
The Forgotten Woman

Monsey
E. Cramer & Sons, Inc.

Merrick
Women's Corner

Newburgh
Dora Dale

New York City
Abraham & Straus
Forgotten Woman

Goldrings Inc.
Lane Bryant
Macy's
Roaman's
Sak's Fifth Avenue
Smart Size
Sydmore Shop

Niagara Falls
James Fashion Shop

Pittsford
Merkel's
 Dept. Store

Richmond Hill
Mayfair Fashions

Rockaway
Sylvia's Corset Closte

Schenectady
The Dunbar Shop, Inc.
Ludeman's

Southampton
Billings Country Shop

Staten Island
Garbers

Valley Stream
For Women Only
Smart Size

Whitehall
Roselli's Clothing

White Plains
Pennington's

NORTH CAROLINA
Added Dimensions

Ahoskie
Belk Dept. Store
John Carroll

Charlotte
J.B. Ivey & Co.

Concord
E.S. Chesson & Sons

Durham
Belk-Legett

Goldsboro
Leder's Dept. Store

Hickory
Tobias, Inc.

Kinston
National of Lexington

Sylva
Adlers of Tarboro

NORTH DAKOTA
Fargo
Herberger, Inc.

Willston
Joseph's

OHIO
Akron
The M. O'Neil Co.
Elizabeths

Beachwood
Julee's

Cincinnati
Lane Bryant
Lowenthals, Inc.
Baron Dept. Store
Francine Bridal & Formal

Cleveland
Bernard H. Freed
The Highbee Co.

Columbus
Sarah Schenck's
Suzanne's

Dayton
Paragon Woman

Logan
Marias Fashions

Mansfield
Cherry Tree

North Olmsted
Markol

Sandusky
Gail's Women's World
Wren's Dept. Store
The Lion Store

Shaker Heights
My Fair Lady

Sylvania
At Last

Youngstown
Strouss'
The V.I.P. Shop

OKLAHOMA
Pawhuska
Diana's Fashion Shop
Queen Fashions

Temple
Froug's, Inc.

Tulsa
Betty Claire's

OREGON
Busham
Big 'N Beautiful Shop

Coos Bay
Emporium

Portland
J. Burton
Castle Fashions
Nordstrom

PENNSYLVANIA
Allentown
Hess Co.
Junior Colony, Inc.

Big &
Beautiful

Altoona
The Dry Goods

Bala-Cynwyd
Jaisons

Donora
Orr's Dept. Store, Inc.

Greenville
Pomeroy's Inc.

Harrisburg
Pomeroy's

Lahaska
Abigail Starr

Philadelphia
Gimbel's
Lane Bryant
Plus Women, Inc.
Strawbridge & Clothier
Wanamaker

Pittsburgh
Joanne's Stout Shoppe
Joseph Horne Co.
Lane Bryant
Kaufman's

Reading
Boscov's

Somerset
The George W. Schenck Co.

RHODE ISLAND
Warwick
Peerless

Big &
Beautiful

230

SOUTH CAROLINA
Added Dimensions

Chester
The Hub, Inc.

Greenwood
The Clothes Line Ltd.

TENNESSEE
Cookeville
Roberson-McMurry-Roberson

Jackson
Zane's

Memphis
Catherine's Stout Shoppes
Goldsmith's
William H. Harris & Co.
Hecht's Tall Shop

Nashville
Sam Shop
Smart Sizes

TEXAS
Abilene
Village Fashions

Amarillo
The Hollywood
Joal's

Beaumont
Adlers Dry Goods

Clarksville
The Hub

Dallas
Joske's
J.C. Penney Co.
Maddox Shop
Sanger-Harris
Sledge's Stylish Stout
Toy Winn

Denton
Craven's Dry Goods

El Paso
Popular

Ft. Worth
Dillard's
Stripling & Cox
Texas Tall & Stout

Gainesville
Pauline's

Galveston
The Woman's Corner

Harlingen
Texas Toggery

Houston
Foley's
Joske's
Women's Shop

Hurst
Young Modern Style

Mt. Vernon
Melba V's

Odessa
Stout Fashions

Pasadena
Jacques Inc.

Port Arthur
Fashions in a Big Way

San Angelo
DBA-Country Elegance Plus

Waco
Career Girl Shops
R.E. Cox Co.

Wichita Falls
Joy's

UTAH
Salt Lake City
Dahle's Queen & Tall
Nordstrom's
Z.C.M.I.

VERMONT
Rutland
The Fashion Show

VIRGINIA
Added Dimensions

Abingdon
Maxine's

Ashland
The Fashion Gal

Bluefield
Magic Mart Stores

Charlottesville
La Grande Dame

Emporia
Bloom Brothers

Falls Church
The Plus Woman

Farmville
Baldwin Stores

Fredericksburgh
Miller's

Gate City
P.H. Nickels

Newport News
La Vogue
Virginia Specialty Shops

Norfolk
J.A. Myers Sons

Richmond
Miller & Rhoads

Springfield
Plus Sizes

Vienna
Plus Sizes

WASHINGTON
Bellevue
Queen Size Boutique

Bremerton
Country Casuals, Inc.

Kennewick
Basin

Seattle
The Bon
Nordstroms
Queen Size Boutique

Spokane
Marjorie's Custom Sizes

WEST VIRGINIA
Charleston
The Diamond
Stone & Thomas

Huntington
Connie Jane's

Wheeling
Good's
Horne's

WISCONSIN
Eau Claire
Del-Maes Apparel

La Crosse
Allen's

Milwaukee
Sizemore Casuals

Racine
Big and Beautiful Woman

TO ORDER BY MAIL:
Great Impressions
720 Anderson Road
St. Cloud, MN 56395

Lady Annabelle Lingerie, Inc.
P.O. Box 1490
Boston, MA 02205

Lane Bryant
Mail Order Division
2300 Southeastern Ave.
P.O. Box 7207
Indianapolis, IN 46272

Nancy's Choice
2300 Southeastern Ave.
Indianapolis, IN 46201

Lane Bryant TALL
    Collection
P.O. Box 7209
2300 Southeastern Ave.
Indianapolis, IN 46207

Roaman's Mail Order
463 Seventh Ave.
New York, NY 10001

The Tog Shop
Lester Square
Americus, GA 31710

Victoria's Secret
395 Sutter Street
San Francisco, CA 94108

2245 Union Street
San Francisco, CA 94123

Index

A
Attitude redirection 38, 174
  changing negative attitudes 46

B
Balance 81
  formal and informal 82
  image 94–101
Before and after myth 65
Big, Beautiful Woman *Magazine* 26, 36, 77, 167
Body fashion trends 126
Body image 50
Body language 63
Body size 50–51

C
Celanese Corp. study 36
Closet organization 38
Clothing value formula 143
Cold reading 53
Color 114
  analysis 113, 116–120
  scheme planning 120
Compulsive eating 182, 184
  controlling compulsive eating 190
Consciousness raising 168
Consumer action 146
Cordova, Coreen 59
Custom made clothes 147

D
Design, good 80, 92
  principles and elements 80
Dieting, a magic cure 34
  doesn't work 181
Dress for Failure Fatphobia Rules 91

E
Emphasis 86
  head 94
  neck 94
  bust 95
  hips 97
  height 98
Europeanization of fashion 130

F
Fabric 113
Fads and cycles 128–129
Fashion, appropriate 131
  high 130
  predicting 128
  silhouette 127
Fat is a feminist issue 26, 165
Fat, days 65
  stereotypes 32, 35
Fatphobia, definition 9
  myths 179
Fatphobia Awareness Training
  groups 169–173
  goals 201
  structure 203–206
  becoming a leader 206–209
  developing a topic 209–211
  discussion questions and
    exercises 212–219
First born/Overachiever syndrome 19

G
Gifted figure 64

H
Harmony 82
Hairstyle 57
Harris, Jeri 158
Hunnicutt, Sandra 19, 163, 169
Health 64

I
Image, development 35
    final exam 149
    goals 68–70
    nonverbal communication 35, 55
    roles 69

L
Less is Best guide 87
Line 82

M
Make over 56
Make-up 59
Medical issues 195–199
Metabolism and genetics 191–192

N
National Association to Aid Fat
    Americans (NAAFA) 36
Natural body weight 187
Nutrition 194

O
Ohearn, Anita 154

P
Personal style 67
Physical image 55
Politte, Jake 56–58
Posture 60
Problem solving 179
Proportion 84

Q
Quality guidelines 132

R
Rhythm 85

S
Scale 85
Self-esteem 39
Self-image 49
Shaw, Carole 36, 60, 147, 180
Smart shopper 138
Smith, Ann 64
Stretch 64
Stylish 67
Super woman image 33

T
Texture 113, 123

U
Unknown fat person exercise 50
Urbanik, Christina 161

V
Visualization 105
Voglino, Adolfo 56
Voice 63

W
Wardrobe plan 140
Worthington, Diane 156

Y
Yin and Yang 70
Yo Yo Syndrome 182

Z
Zoftig 56, 156, 158

Big &
Beautiful

233

Credits

Models
Special Thanks To:
Clementina De Pena, *Anita Ohearn Productions,* Lafayette, California; p. 12, 154, plate A
Alicia Johnson, *Sabina Agency,* San Francisco, California; p. 8, 11, plate D and E
Barbara Grand, *Sabina Agency,* San Francisco, California; Plate J
Linda Savarese, Walnut Creek, California, p. 2, Plate A and K
Teddy Williams, *Sabina Agency,* San Francisco, California; p. 10, plate F and G
Kelly Williams; *Scott Agency,* San Francisco, California; p. 61, 84, 96, 102, 133, Plate H and I

Clothing
Added Dimensions;
  Walnut Creek, California
Plate A—Wine knit skirt, bold print sweater, and off-white jacket from Rejoice
Plate J—Cherry sweater—Bonnie Lee Le roy, Green Jacket—Action Country Skirt—Half Time Blouse—Lucky Me Pants—Rejoice
Plate K—Jacket and skirt, wine sweater and knit skirt—Rejoice

Zoftig; San Francisco, California
Page 2—Pat Davis designer for Summer and Winter features loom woven Ruana. Blouse and pant by Bobbie June.
Page 8—Designer Ruth Bowden teal waterfall coat and harem pant. Jon Scott silk ruffle blouse
Page 10—Carmen "G" swing coat and harem pant jumpsuit in raspberry
Page 12 and *Plate A*—Wine tunic and straight leg pant by Carole Koch designer of French Vanilla. Hand died silk Turkish style coat by Judith Content.

Lane Bryant (Mail Order)

Photo Processing
Don Twitchell, *Custom Color;* Pleasant Hill, California

Photographer
Jon W. Olds, *Image Communication Co.;* Concord, California
Leroy Goodenough, Photo assistant
Ruthanne Olds, Fashion Coordinator and Photo Stylist

Photo Credits
Page 1; David Neely, *Photo Concepts,* Washington, D.C. (model, Lyn Green, *Anne Schwab's Model Store,* Washington, D.C.) Page 2; Jon Olds. Page 5; Jon Olds. Page 6; David Neely (model, Wendy Davidson, *Anne Schwab's Model Store,* Washington, D.C.) Page 7; David Neely. Pages 8-10-12; Jon Olds. Page 30; Stout Sportswear Group, 1411 Broadway, New York, NY 10018 (photographer, William Benedict, Inc., 5 Tudor City Place, New York, NY). Page 42; Lane Bryant, 11 West 42nd Street, New York, NY 10036. Page 52; Stout Sportswear Group. Page 61; Jon Olds. Page 74; Stout Sportswear Group. Page 84; Jon Olds. Page 90; Lane Bryant. Page 96; Jon Olds. Page 99; Lane Bryant. Page 101; Jon Olds. Page 104; *Lingerie:* Lady Annabelle Lingerie, Inc., P.O. Box 1490, Boston MA 02205, *Advertising Agency:* Maslow, Gold & Rothschild, Inc., 1220 Statler Office Building, Boston, MA 02116, *Photography:* Robert Barclay Studios, New York, NY. Page 124; Stout Sportswear Group. Page 133; Jon Olds. Page 136; Stout Sportswear Group. Page 152; Lane Bryant. Page 154; Jon Olds. Page 156; Jon Olds. Page 159; Jon Olds. Page 161; Jon Olds. Page 164; Jon Olds. Page 166; Lane Bryant. Page 171; Jon Olds. Page 178; Lane Bryant. Page 200; Lady Annabelle Lingerie, Inc. Page 220; Stout Sportswear Group.

Color Plates A-K; Jon Olds. Color Plate L; Lane Bryant.

Illustrations
Allyson Everngam

Artists
Leslie Eichner
Allyson Everngam
David Uslan

Ask for a free "THIN'S NOT IN" button at your booksellers. It's free with your purchase of a copy of Big & Beautiful for yourself and friends you want to help overcome "fat-phobia" or with your purchase of any of the following fashion and image books.

Color Me Beautiful
Discover Your Natural Beauty through Color

by Carole Jackson

Although paperback edition has 700,000 copies in print, this hardcover gift edition, is now in its sixth printing!

Called "A Big Girl's Coloring Book" by *King Features'* Joan O'Sullivan, this fascinating book tells you how—without dieting or effort—you can be more totally beautiful through color today!

With 700,000 copies now in print, this book's secret to instant beauty through color has intrigued women all over the world. Here is some of the praise

"Color is the name of the most basic beauty game in town. And if you don't know how to play, fashion consultant Carole Jackson has compiled all the rules in a new book, Color Me Beautiful." —*The New York Daily News*

"Color Me Beautiful outlines a do-it-yourself color analysis method based on an interpretation of natural skintones." —*The Los Angeles Times*

ISBN 87491-281-4/$14.95
hardcover gift edition
212 pages, 8×9, illustrated, full color photos

Choices of a Growing Woman

by Maggie S. Davis

Blooming is a woman-to-woman book about choices. The book is a testimony to the author's belief that no matter how much money a woman makes, no matter what her age or state of mind, she can always choose to start moving in directions that feel better to her.

Each chapter is not a chapter—but an exploration of a specific choice . . .

Choice #1: To Believe in My Own Power

Choice #2: To Treat Myself Royally

Choice #3: To Reach Out to Others

Choice #4: To Stop Sabotaging My Decisions

Choice #5: To Take Risks

Choice #6: To Forget My Age

Maggie Davis, a doctor's daughter, has been a mediator, counslor, trainer, teacher, waitress, poet, editor, writer.

ISBN 87491-418-3/$8.95
hardcover
132 pages, 5½×8½, illustrated

Working Wardrobe
Affordable Clothes that Work for You!

by Janet Wallach

". . . A new fashion math based on a 'Capsule Concept' worked out by a noted fashion authority, Janet Wallach." —*Modern Bride*

". . . what to wear where . . . how-to for career women." —*New York Post*

"Five Easy Pieces . . . At Work" —*The Washington Post*

"This book can really save you money!" —*Tom Martin, AP Radio Network*

Working Wardrobe addresses the fifty percent of all adult American women who work full time. All of them want to dress to reflect their own self-image—and the image they wish to create—but they frequently lack the time to build an exciting wardrobe.

Now in *Working Wardrobe* noted designer and fashion director, Janet Wallach, explains her "Capsule Concept," an easy affordable way to build a wardrobe that works for you.

ISBN 87491-072-2/$14.95
hardcover
212 pages, 8×9, illustrated, color

If your bookseller does not have these titles, send your check or money order for the price of the book plus $1.50 for postage and handling to: **Acropolis Books Ltd., 2400 17th Street, N.W., Washington, D.C. 20009 or call toll-free 800–621–5199.** If you want to order only a "THIN'S NOT IN" button, send Acropolis a stamped, self addressed envelope, plus 25¢. We'll see you get your button right away.

If you want to order only a
"THIN'S NOT IN" button, send Acropolis a stamped, self addressed
envelope, plus 25¢. We'll see you get your button right away.

ACROPOLIS BOOKS LTD.
2400 17th Street, N.W.
Washington, D.C. 20009

BB Femme
Beautiful Big Woman